The Battle of Hastings

Books in the Battles Series:

✠ Battles of the Middle Ages ✠

The Battle of Hastings

by William W. Lace

Lucent Books, P.O. Box 289011, San Diego, CA 92198-9011

Library of Congress Cataloging-in-Publication Data

Lace, William W.
    The Battle of Hastings / by William W. Lace.
     p. cm. — (Battles of the Middle Ages)
    Includes bibliographical references and index.
    ISBN 1-56006-416-1 (Lib. ed. : alk. paper)
    1. Hastings, Battle of, 1066—Juvenile literature. [1. Hastings,
Battle of, 1066. 2. Great Britain—History—William I, 1066-1087.]
I. Title. II. Series.
DA196.L33 1996
942.02'1—dc20
                                                   95-11711
                                                      CIP
                                                      AC

Contents

Foreword

Almost everyone would agree with William Tecumseh Sherman that war "is all hell." Yet the history of war, and battles in particular, is so fraught with the full spectrum of human emotion and action that it becomes a microcosm of the human experience. Soldiers' lives are condensed and crystallized in a single battle. As Francis Miller explains in his *Photographic History of the Civil War* when describing the war wounded, "It is sudden, the transition from marching bravely at morning on two sound legs, grasping your rifle in two sturdy arms, to lying at nightfall under a tree with a member forever gone."

Decisions made on the battlefield can mean the lives of thousands. A general's pique or indigestion can result in the difference between life and death. Some historians speculate, for example, that Napoleon's fateful defeat at Waterloo was due to the beginnings of stomach cancer. His stomach pain may have been the reason that the normally decisive general was sluggish and reluctant to move his troops. And what kept George McClellan from winning battles during the Civil War? Some scholars and contemporaries believe that it was simple cowardice and fear. Others argue that he felt a gut-wrenching unwillingness to engage in the war of attrition that was characteristic of that particular conflict.

Battle decisions can be magnificently brilliant and horribly costly. At the Battle of Thaspus in 47 B.C., for example, Julius Caesar, facing a numerically superior army, shrewdly ordered his troops onto a narrow strip of land bordering the sea. Just as he expected, his enemy thought he had accidentally trapped himself and divided their forces to surround his troops. By dividing their army, his enemy had given Caesar the strategic edge he needed to defeat them. Other battle orders result in disaster, as in the case of the Battle at Balaklava during the Crimean War in 1854. A British general gave the order to attack a force of withdrawing enemy Russians. But confusion in relaying the order resulted in the 670 men of the Light Brigade's charging in the wrong direction into certain death by heavy enemy cannon fire. Battles are the stuff of history on the grandest scale—their outcomes often determine whether nations are enslaved or liberated.

Moments in battles illustrate the best and worst of human character. In the feeling of terror and the us-versus-them attitude that accompanies war, the enemy can be dehumanized and treated with a contempt that is considered repellent in times of peace. At Wounded Knee, the distrust and anticipation of violence that grew between the Native Americans and American soldiers led to the senseless killing of ninety men, women, and children. And who can forget My Lai, where the deaths of old men, women, and children at the hands of American soldiers shocked an America already disillusioned with the Vietnam War. The murder of six million Jews will remain burned into the human conscience forever as the measure of man's inhumanity to man. These horrors cannot be forgotten. And yet, under the terrible conditions of battle, one can find acts of bravery, kindness, and altruism. During the Battle of Midway, the members of Torpedo Squadron 8, flying in hope-lessly antiquated planes and without the benefit of air protection from fighters, tried bravely to fulfill their mission—to destroy the *Kido Butai,* the Japanese Carrier Striking Force. Without air sup-port, the squadron was immediately set upon by Japanese fighters. Nevertheless, each bomber tried valiantly to hit his target. Each failed. Every man but one died in the effort. But by keeping the Japanese fighters busy, the squadron bought time and delayed fur-ther Japanese fighter attacks. In the aftermath of the Battle of Isan-dhlwana in South Africa in 1879, a force of thousands of Zulu war-riors trapped a contingent of British troops in a small trading post. After repeated bloody attacks in which many died on both sides, the Zulus, their final victory certain, granted the remaining British their lives as a gesture of respect for their bravery. During World War I, American troops were so touched by the fate of French war orphans that they took up a collection to help them. During the Civil War, soldiers of the North and South would briefly forget that they were enemies and share smokes and coffee across battle lines during the endless nights. These acts seem all the more dra-matic, more uplifting, because they indicate that people can con-tinue to behave with humanity when faced with inhumanity.

Lucent Books' Battles Series highlights the vast range of the human character revealed in the ordeal of war. Dramatic narra-tive describes in exciting and accurate detail the commanders, soldiers, weapons, strategies, and maneuvers involved in each battle. Each volume includes a comprehensive historical context, explaining what brought the parties to war, the events leading to the battle, what factors made the battle important, and the effects it had on the larger war and later events.

The Battles Series also includes a chronology of important dates that gives students an overview, at a glance, of each battle. Sidebars create a broader context by adding enlightening details on leaders, institutions, customs, warships, weapons, and armor mentioned in the narration. Every volume contains numerous maps that allow readers to better visualize troop movements and strategies. In addition, numerous primary and secondary source quotations drawn from both past historical witnesses and modern historians are included. These quotations demonstrate to readers how and where historians derive information about past events. Finally, the volumes in the Battles Series provide a launching point for further reading and research. Each book contains a bibliography designed for student research, as well as a second bibliography that includes the works the author consulted while compiling the book.

Above all, the Battles Series helps illustrate the words of Herodotus, the fifth-century B.C. Greek historian now known as the "father of history." In the opening lines of his great chronicle of the Greek and Persian Wars, the world's first battle book, he set for himself this goal: "To preserve the memory of the past by putting on record the astonishing achievements both of our own and of other peoples; and more particularly, to show how they came into conflict."

Chronology of Events

700–300 B.C.
Celts invade Britain.

55 B.C.
Invasion of Britain by Roman general Julius Caesar.

A.D. 43
Invasion of Britain under Roman emperor Claudius I.

449
Beginning of Anglo-Saxon invasions.

789
First appearance of Danes in England.

A Viking ship sports the characteristic dragon as a bowhead.

836
Beginning of frequent Danish raids.

851
Danes begin year-round occupation.

878
Defeat of Guthrum at Edington by English king Alfred the Great.

898
Vikings settle in what would become Normandy.

899
Death of Alfred the Great.

911
Rolf is acknowledged the ruler of Normandy by King Charles III of France.

937
Defeat of the Danes at Brunanburh by Athelstan.

965
Peace of Gisors brings Normandy and France closer together.

981
Renewal of Danish invasion in England.

991
Pope arranges treaty between Normandy and England.

1002
Marriage of Emma, sister of Richard II of Normandy, to King Ethelred of England.

1013
Invasion of England by King Sweyn Forkbeard of Denmark.

1017
Canute becomes king of England.

ca. 1027
Birth of William the Conqueror in Falaise, Normandy.

1035
Death of Canute; death of Duke Robert I of Normandy, father of William the Conqueror.

1036
Murder of Prince Alfred, son of Ethelred, at the command of Godwin of Wessex.

1042
Death of King Hardecanute of England; Edward the Confessor becomes king.

1046
Guy of Burgundy leads rebellion against William.

The Normans sack England.

1047

Battle of Val-és-Dunes is won by William; Harald Hardraade becomes king of Norway.

1051

Marriage of Duke William and Matilda of Flanders; Godwin of Wessex is banished from England by King Edward.

1052

Edward names William his heir; Godwin returns to power in England.

1054

Battle of Mortemer is won by William's troops.

1057

Battle of Varaville is won by William.

1064

Harold of Wessex swears to uphold William's claim to throne of England.

1065

Harold's brother, Tostig, is banished from England.

1066

January 5   Death of King Edward the Confessor of England.

January 6   Coronation of King Harold in Westminster Abbey.

February   William attempts to gain support of Norman nobles at Council of Lillebonne.

April   William begins to build invasion fleet.

June   English army called up by Harold.

August   Harald Hardraade's fleet leaves Norway.

September 8   Harold dismisses army, recalls fleet to London.

September 12   William's fleet moves to Saint Valéry.

September 19   Harald Hardraade's fleet lands at Riccal, an English village.

September 20   Harald Hardraade defeats Morcar and Edwin at Fulford Gate.

September 25   Harald Hardraade is defeated and killed by Harold of England at the Battle of Stamford Bridge.

September 27   William's fleet sails from Saint Valéry and lands at Pevensey in England the next morning.

October 5   Harold and his army arrive back in London.

October 12   Harold and his army begin the march from London to Hastings.

October 14   Battle of Hastings is won by William the Conqueror; King Harold of England is killed.

December 25   William is crowned king of England in Westminster Abbey.

INTRODUCTION

When History Reaches a Crossroad

This book, the story of the Battle of Hastings, is one in a series on important battles in history. The question, then, may be asked: is there such a thing as an unimportant battle? Any armed conflict—whether a clash of massive armies or a skirmish between platoons—is of prime importance to those who fight in it and who might lose their lives. The smallest battle, whatever its impact on the war, certainly is important to the farmer across whose fields tanks roll or the townsman whose home is bombed to rubble.

If no battle is unimportant, it perhaps is necessary to use another word to describe those monumental conflicts that find their way into history books and that make up this series. One such word would be *crucial,* derived from the Latin word for cross. Indeed, the truly important battle should be one in which historical events come to a crossroad. The battle should have not only a decisive impact on the war, but also a similar impact on history. It should decide which direction history takes.

Not all important battles are crucial. The Battle of Gettysburg during the American Civil War was important but not decisive. The North's manpower and industrial output would eventually have enabled it to win the war even if the South had won at Gettysburg. The great battles of World War II, such as Stalingrad in the USSR and Midway in the Pacific Ocean, surely hastened the end of the war, but the outcome had essentially been decided when the United States joined the alliance against the overextended Germans and Japanese.

A Turn in the Road

Also, in order for a battle to be crucial, it should be one in which not only history, but also the outcome of the battle itself hangs in the balance—when there is an equal chance of a turn at the crossroad one way or another. Such was the situation a little less than a thousand years ago when William of Normandy and Harold II of England met on October 14, 1066, just north of the English seaport of Hastings. The two armies were almost evenly matched. The battle was a close, hard-fought encounter lasting all day. Victory could have gone to the English just as easily as to the Normans. Both commanders had risked everything on this single encounter. There would be no second chance, no tomorrow. It was a winner-take-all situation.

Perhaps the last such decisive conflict was the Battle of Britain, fought between the British and German air forces in 1940. The result hung in the balance for months. Either side could have won. A German victory would likely have led to a successful invasion of Great Britain, and the United States might never have entered the war.

The days of crucial battles, of titanic, or enormous, struggles in which history reaches a turning point, may be in the past. Warfare has become too complex, too spread out, too technical. One cannot point to any battle in the Gulf War, Vietnam War, or Korean War as having been the decisive point. Many troops representing many countries fight on fronts stretching hundreds of miles.

Warfare was much simpler and much more decisive in 1066. There were only two generals, two armies, and one battle—The Battle of Hastings. It would change the course of history not only for England, but for the rest of the world.

William the Conqueror views the Battle of Hastings from atop his horse.

CHAPTER ONE

The Making of England

William, duke of Normandy (a part of France), conquered England in 1066 by defeating King Harold at the Battle of Hastings. It was the last time a foreign power has ever successfully invaded England, but it was by no means the first. The British Isles had a long record, stretching much further back than recorded history, of being overrun from mainland Europe.

In earliest times there was not even the English Channel to hinder invaders. Britain, not yet an island, was joined to the European continent. The Thames River flowed not into the sea, but into the Rhine River. For centuries tribes of hunters wandered back and forth across a land bridge in search of game.

Eventually, from the melting of huge glaciers, the sea rose, and the British Isles were formed. That did not stop the flow of immigration and invasion. For one thing, Britain was easy to invade. The English Channel is narrow—only twelve miles at the narrowest point. For another, the southern coast of Britain has plenty of natural harbors, and foreign armies, once ashore, found the gently rolling land ideal for marching. And once an army was on the march, no geographical barriers existed to stop it before it reached the mountains of Wales far to the west or the Highlands of Scotland far to the north.

The first invasion about which much is known began about 700 B.C. and continued in waves over the next four hundred years. The earliest inhabitants of Britain—short, dark skinned, and called by scientists the Iberians—were conquered by a tall, fair-haired people known as the Celts. The Celts consisted of many tribes, one of which—the Brythons—was to give the island its name, Britain. The Celtic civilization was more advanced, with iron weapons instead of bronze, which featured intricate gold ornaments. The Iberians were pushed back far to the west and north.

The Britons, as all the Celtic tribes eventually came to be known, never formed anything that resembled a nation. There were no territorial boundaries. The tribes were constantly at war with one another. The only time they came together was against a common enemy.

Caesar and the Romans

That enemy made its first appearance in the person of Julius Caesar, the Roman general who had conquered the Celtic tribes in Gaul, now France. Caesar's first invasion, in 55 B.C., was a failure. He landed near what is now the city of Dover and was able to move inland only about ten miles before being driven back to his ships. He had better luck the next year, winning several battles and capturing a quantity of gold and several slaves.

Uprisings in Gaul and civil war within the Roman Empire gave Britain a hundred years free from invasion. Then, in A.D. 43, the legions of the Roman emperor Claudius I invaded and eventually conquered the entire island, except for Scotland.

The Romans sail toward the English coast.

For more than four hundred years Britain was a Roman colony. The Romans built the first London Bridge across the Thames and a network of roads, the courses of which are still followed by English highways. They built forts around which cities sprang up. Such names as Winchester, Manchester, and Lancaster come from *castrum*, the Latin word for fort.

Although the tribes in Wales and in the far north remained troublesome and rebellious, most Britons accepted Roman rule and adopted Roman ways, wearing togas, living in villas, and speaking Latin. Christianity was introduced, although it did not become widespread during that era. The Britons were peaceful, contented, and over the centuries became a people far removed from the warriors who had conquered the Iberians.

The Britons' complacency posed no danger as long as the Roman legions protected the Britons from the wilder tribes, especially the Picts and the Scots in the north, and from raids by pirates from a northern German tribe known as the Saxons. But by the early fifth century, the Roman Empire began to shrink. The legions that were needed to repel foreign invaders and deal with revolts at home were gradually withdrawn from Britain, and the Britons were on their own.

As the Romans left, the wild tribes increased their attacks on the wealthy cities and farms of central and south Britain. The Britons, no longer able to defend themselves, were forced to hire warriors from Germany and Denmark to help them. Eventually the very people the Britons brought in as allies would take over most of the island and establish an Anglo-Saxon England.

The Dark Ages

It is at this point in history that the British Isles entered what is known as the Dark Ages, which were to last until about 1200, long after the Battle of Hastings. These were not, as is sometimes supposed, centuries of complete barbarism. On the contrary, art and learning took place. Architecture flourished. The foundations of modern Europe were laid.

The reference to the word *dark* stems from a lack of written records. Only a handful of documents from that era have survived. Most of those were written by monks who were not directly involved in events and who, in some cases, were writing centuries after the events. The people they write about, the places they describe, may be real or may be folk legends. As David Howarth wrote in his book about the Norman Conquest, "Strictly speaking, any sentence in a story nine centuries old should include the word *perhaps*; nothing is completely certain."

Certainly this is the case with the Anglo-Saxon invasion of Britain. According to the *Anglo-Saxon Chronicle*, a Briton chief named Vortigern invited brothers Hengest and Horsa, chiefs of

In this fanciful painting taken from a larger work, a monk works on a manuscript as the events that he writes about take place outside his window. The events of the Battle of Hastings were written down by monks, who were among the few who could read and write.

Angle chiefs Hengest and Horsa and their warriors are welcomed to England by Briton chief Vortigern. Invited to help Vortigern, Hengest and Horsa decided to turn on him and take over England themselves.

the Angles in southern Denmark, to come to his aid against the Picts in 449. They did so but soon realized that the land could be theirs for the taking. They sent messengers home, telling "of the worthlessness of the Britons and of the excellence of the land."

Soon, the *Chronicle* says, more warriors descended on Britain. They came not to help the Britons, but to conquer them. "First, they slew the enemies of the king [Vortigern] and drove them away, and afterwards they turned against the king and against the Britons and destroyed them by fire and by the edge of the sword."

The Britons were not exactly as worthless as the *Chronicle* might suggest. The Anglo-Saxon conquest lasted more than 150 years and was never fully completed. A British monk named Gildas wrote of a great victory by the Britons under King Arthur at Mount Badon, but the site of the battle has never been identified, and Arthur remains more legendary than real.

The Saxons land on the shores of England. Such tribes would eventually drive out most of the original inhabitants of the area.

Description of Destruction

Eventually, however, like the Iberians, the Britons were driven north into Scotland and west into Wales. Gildas in the mid–sixth century wrote:

> Every colony [town] is leveled to the ground by the stroke of the battering ram. The inhabitants are slaughtered along with the guardians of their churches, priests, and people alike, while the sword gleamed on every side, and the flames crackled around. . . . Of the miserable remnant some flee to the hills, only to be captured and slain in heaps; some, constrained [limited] by famine, come in and surrender themselves to be slaves for ever to the enemy. . . . Others, wailing, pass bitterly overseas.

Some of the Britons, indeed, fled across the English Channel to western France, settling in the area that has been known ever since as Brittany.

The English monk Bede, writing his *Ecclesiastical History of the English People* in the eighth century, divided the conquerors into three tribes—the Saxons from northern Germany, the Jutes from Jutland in Denmark, and the Angles, who he said were from an area between the Saxons and the Jutes. The Saxons settled mostly in the southern part of Britain; the Jutes, in the southeast; and the Angles, in the north.

Like the Britons before them, the invaders were not unified. Instead of tribal areas, they formed kingdoms with rough boundaries. Their rulers were more like the kings of later times than tribal chiefs. There was no England, as such, even though the new settlers began to be known collectively as the English, from the word *Angles*. The seven kingdoms making up what historians called the heptarchy were Kent, Northumbria, Mercia, East Anglia, and the three Saxon kingdoms—Essex, Sussex, and Wessex (or, east Saxons, south Saxons, west Saxons).

Other, smaller kingdoms—Elmet, Deira, Bernicia, and Lindsey—grew up from time to time but were swallowed by their larger neighbors. Actually, by the year 600 only three of the seven—Northumbria, Mercia, and Wessex—were powerful enough to influence the others. The kingdoms were constantly at war, with first one, then another gaining supremacy, or authority.

The Anglo-Saxon Kingdoms, Sixth Century

The Horse in Warfare

Horses were introduced as weapons of war in Britain by the Roman general Julius Caesar. After Caesar's first expedition to Britain ended in failure in 55 B.C., he tried again the next year. This time he brought a force of two thousand cavalrymen, or mounted soldiers, from Gaul, now France, and was far more successful.

The Celtic tribes who fought against Caesar adopted the use of horses, but their native ponies were far too small to be used for a massed charge. Instead the Celts used horsemen for hit-and-run attacks. Later, during the revolt of the Celts under Queen Boudicca in the first century A.D., the Celts copied the Romans by hitching horses to chariots.

The use of horses in battle died out completely under the Anglo-Saxons, who began their invasion of Britain in about 450. Like the Scandinavians, who began invasions of their own in the late eighth century, the Anglo-Saxons rode horses to the sites of battles but fought on foot. Again, the reason was that the native horses were too small.

At the Battle of Hastings, however, the Norman invaders continued their long tradition of fighting on horseback. Over many years they had developed a breed of large war horses strong enough to carry armored warriors into battle. The mobility of Duke William and Normandy's cavalry was one of the deciding factors at the Battle of Hastings.

The Cruelty of War

Warfare between the kingdoms was violent. Although the English—who originally worshiped a host of Germanic gods such as Odin and Thor—were gradually converted to Christianity over the centuries, they remained fierce and cruel in battle and even in victory. Prominent prisoners often were blinded or killed to remove them as future threats. In 789, for example, a man named Ethelred seized Northumbria and secured his throne by having the surviving sons of the former king drowned.

The year 789 was considerably more significant because of an event far to the south. Three ships landed near Dorchester on the coast of Wessex. A representative of King Beorhtric rode to meet them. As the *Anglo-Saxon Chronicle* relates, the official "tried to compel them to go to the royal manor, for he did not know what they were, and they slew him. These were the first ships of the Danes to come to England." It was an isolated incident, but it marked the beginning of yet another invasion of Britain. This one, by the Danes, would last more than 250 years and end only days before the Battle of Hastings.

Historians are not sure what factors led to the explosion of exploration and conquest by the Scandinavian peoples in the ninth century. Some think that political unity after centuries of civil warfare was the root cause. Others say the population had increased beyond the ability of the land to produce food, so that foreign adventures were necessary. Still others claim the lust for adventure had always been there but that improvements in shipbuilding finally made it possible.

Whatever the causes, the result was dramatic. Warriors from Norway, Denmark, and Sweden pushed their way not only into England, but also as far west as North America and as far east as Constantinople on the edge of the Mediterranean Sea. They came to be known as Vikings, or creek dwellers, from the word *vik*, which means "creek." They sailed from the inlets and fjords of their own lands to terrorize much of Europe, whose people lived in dread of the long ships surmounted by figureheads of dragons.

Recurring Raids

England was free from such attacks for about forty years after that initial appearance in 789, but in 836 Scandinavian pirates ravaged the Isle of Sheppey in the mouth of the Thames River. They discovered that the coast was mostly undefended and that the English had no sea force to oppose them. Thereafter, almost every spring the raiders—all known as Danes by the English, even if they might have been Norwegians—appeared, rowing their ships far up rivers and marching across land. Sometimes they were defeated, but they often won, carrying gold and slaves

The Vikings (or Danes) disembark on the English coast to begin raiding and pillaging. Most of the time, the Vikings were satisfied with raiding the coastal villages, not attempting a land invasion until 865.

back home. Many an entry in the *Anglo-Saxon Chronicle* ends with the words "and the Danes had possession of the place of slaughter."

The pattern was broken in 851 when the Danes, rather than sailing away with their booty, took up quarters for the winter on the Isle of Thanet just off the southeastern coast. Four years later another Danish army wintered at Sheppey. What had been a series of hit-and-run raids had become an invasion.

In 865 a large Danish force led by brothers Halfdene and Ivar the Boneless landed in East Anglia. The people there quickly

Queen Boudicca

The first recorded heroine of Britain was Boudicca, wife of Prasutagus, the king of the Iceni, one of the tribes of Britons. During the conquest of Britain by the Romans that began in A.D. 54, the king attempted to save the Iceni from destruction by making the Roman emperor, Claudius, his heir.

The Roman legions serving under Suetonius, the governor, paid no attention and overran the Iceni. The king was killed, Boudicca was publicly whipped, and her two daughters were raped by soldiers.

Humiliated and outraged, Boudicca convinced the surviving Iceni to revolt. The rebellion began in A.D. 60 and quickly spread to other tribes. Soon all of southern Britain was up in arms. Londinium, now London, and Camulodunum, now Colchester, were burned to the ground.

Boudicca, described as having flaming red hair, drove her chariot from tribe to tribe, urging the men to fight. "We British are used to women commanders in war," she cried. "I am descended from mighty men. But I am not fighting for my kingdom and wealth now. I am fighting as an ordinary person for my lost freedom, my bruised body, and my outraged daughters."

Suetonius, however, marched against the rebels with ten thousand veteran troops and massacred them. Some eighty thousand Britons were killed, as opposed to four hundred Romans. Boudicca, seeing her cause lost, poisoned herself. She is honored today with a statue near the houses of Parliament in London.

Queen Boudicca urges the people to defend their country against the Roman invaders.

surrendered and agreed to provide the invaders with all they required, including horses. Now able to strike quickly and at greater distances, the Danes attacked Northumbria, capturing the capital city of York in 866. Within a few years Mercia also fell, and of the English kingdoms, only Wessex remained.

Two things saved Wessex, and the English, from being completely overrun. First, the Danish army was divided into two parts. The southern arm, commanded by a king named Guthrum, attacked Wessex. Second, the English found a savior in King Alfred of Wessex, later known as Alfred the Great.

At first Alfred had no more success against the Danes than did the other English kings. He was barely able to avoid defeat and, during the winter of 877–878, he was forced to go into hiding in the marshes far to the west of his capital of Winchester. From his sanctuary he coordinated small raids against the Danes, and in the summer of 878 he gathered an army and defeated Guthrum at Edington. Guthrum agreed to be baptized a Christian and to remove his army from Wessex. Eventually a formal border was established that extended from the Thames northwest to the Welsh border. The area to the north and east of this line was known as the Danelaw, that is, where the Danes ruled.

Alfred's Successors

Alfred the Great has been called the first true king of England, but that was premature. Alfred died in 899, but his son Edward continued his father's struggle. Under Edward, his remarkable sister Ethelfleda—who directed the forces of Mercia after her husband, the king, died—and his son Athelstan, the Danelaw was reconquered. In 937 Athelstan defeated a Danish army on a battlefield of uncertain location named Brunanburh. For the first time a single person was acknowledged as king over all England.

This united kingdom would not last long. Athelstan died in 939 and was succeeded in turn by his brothers Edmund and Edred and then by Edmund's sons, Edwy and Edgar. All had to face rebellions by the Danish population but managed to keep Athelstan's kingdom intact. When Edgar died in 975, he left two sons, Edward and Ethelred. They were only boys of thirteen and nine, and soon each was surrounded by supporters hoping to rule

Alfred the Great, deemed by some to be the first true English king, succeeded in keeping the Danes from conquering Wessex.

Hadrian's Wall

The Romans conquered Britain and maintained it as a colony for more than four hundred years. Despite repeated attempts by their mighty legions, however, they were never able to take Scotland.

After one particularly bloody defeat in the year 121, the Roman emperor Hadrian made a personal inspection. He decided that Scotland was not worth the trouble and should be abandoned. But to prevent raids by the wild tribes of Picts and Scots, he ordered a fortified wall built.

Called Hadrian's Wall, it stretched seventy-three miles from the mouth of the Tyne River in the east to the Solway Firth, or inlet, in the west. It was completed in only five years and was eight feet thick and about twenty feet high. There were sixteen major forts along its length and numerous smaller forts, or mile castles, so-called because they were about a mile apart.

On the north side of the wall the Romans dug a thirty-foot trench to slow any attack. On the south side ran a wide, smooth, straight road. When any part of the wall was under attack, Roman soldiers lit signal fires on top of the wall, and reinforcements marched quickly down the road to help.

Hadrian's Wall accomplished its purpose. Britain was safe from northern raiders until the legions began to be withdrawn early in the fifth century. Although many of the stones have been taken by farmers for use in walls through the centuries, long sections of the wall are still in place and remain an outstanding example of Roman engineering.

Remnants of Hadrian's Wall, originally built in 121, still stand today.

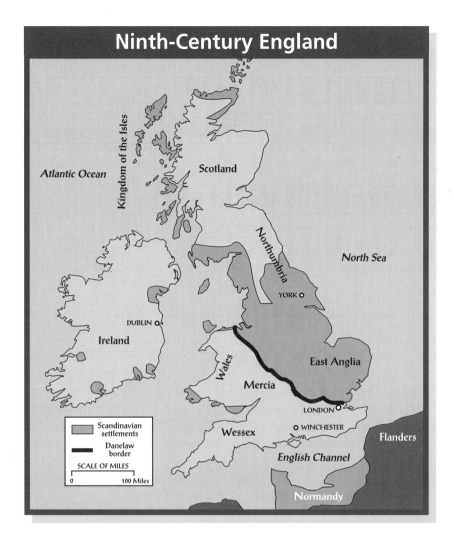

Ninth-Century England

Atlantic Ocean

Kingdom of the Isles

Scotland

North Sea

Northumbria

YORK O

DUBLIN O

Ireland

Wales

East Anglia

Mercia

LONDON O

Wessex

O WINCHESTER

Flanders

English Channel

Normandy

Scandinavian settlements

Danelaw border

SCALE OF MILES

0   100 Miles

through them. Edward was crowned king but in 978 was murdered by followers of Ethelred.

Ethelred is known to history as the Unready, because his reign witnessed the loss of everything Alfred had gained. Ethelred means, in Anglo-Saxon, "noble counsel." During his lifetime Ethelred was given the nickname "Unred," which actually means "no counsel," rather than "unready." This may be either because he had bad advice or simply refused to listen to good advice. Either way, he was unready for what happened and unlucky that it began just after he became king. After a long period of internal strife, the Danes began to raid in force in 981.

CHAPTER TWO

Normandy and Duke William

The Scandinavian invasions of the ninth century were by no means limited to England. The coast of France was just as vulnerable to attack as was the coast of England. Indeed, a feature of the ninth and tenth centuries was that when resistance increased on one side of the English Channel, the Vikings would simply move to the other side. And it was in France that the Vikings established the state that would eventually produce the victor of the Battle of Hastings.

In about 898, chased from England by Alfred the Great, a small force of Scandinavians landed near the mouth of the Seine River in France. Over the next decade they took control of a large area on either side of the river. The details of their conquest are unknown, but in 911 their leader, Rolf—called Rollo by the French—met with the French king, Charles III, the Simple. Rolf was given formal rule over the area, which would thereafter be known as Normandy, or place of the Northmen, or Norsemen.

The newcomers proved to be troublesome. For more than fifty years there were wars between the Norman dukes and the French kings. Finally, in 965 a peace treaty was made in Normandy at Gisors.

Following the Peace of Gisors the Normans rapidly lost their Viking heritage and became Frenchmen. Their language and customs became almost indistinguishable from those in other parts of France. The pagan religion of Scandinavia was forgotten, and Normandy became a center for the establishment of Christian monasteries.

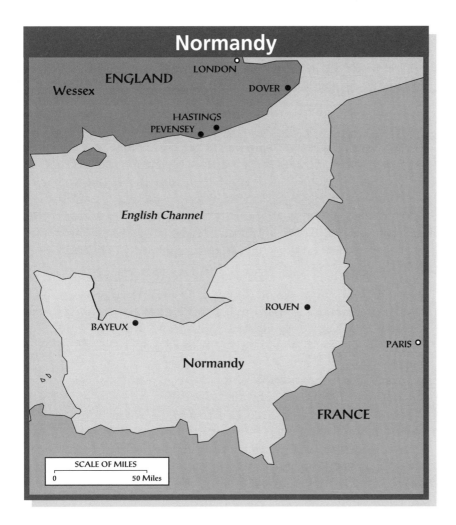

Normandy

ENGLAND
Wessex
LONDON
DOVER
HASTINGS
PEVENSEY
English Channel
ROUEN
BAYEUX
PARIS
Normandy
FRANCE

SCALE OF MILES
0   50 Miles

Still, the Normans had not completely forgotten their northern kin. After the Danes renewed their attacks on England in 981, Normans sometimes gave shelter to Danish ships in their ports and furnished the Danes with food. When King Ethelred of England complained to the pope in 991, the pope negotiated a treaty whereby both England and Normandy pledged never to help one another's enemies. When it was clear by 1002 that something more than a treaty was needed, Ethelred married Emma, who was the sister of the Norman duke Richard II and the great-granddaughter of Rolf. This marriage was to firmly intertwine the fates of Normandy and England and was one of the key events leading to the Battle of Hastings.

Sweyn's Invasion

The marriage, however, came too late to save England. In 1003 the Danes' quest for plunder became a war of conquest. King Sweyn Forkbeard himself led an invading army and for the next ten years spread periodic destruction throughout England. Only

King Sweyn Forkbeard (above) conquered England in 1013, forcing King Ethelred to escape to Normandy. Unfortunately, Sweyn did not live to enjoy his victory and was killed by an unknown hand in 1014.

huge sums of danegeld, a tax raised to buy off the Danish invaders, bought the English any temporary relief. Ethelred had proved to be an incompetent general, and the English were beginning to despair. One chronicler complained:

> When the enemy was in the east, then our levies [troops] were mustered in the west; and when they were in the south, then our levies were in the north. Then all the councilors were summoned to the king, for a plan for the defence of the realm had to be devised then and there, but whatever course of action was decided upon it was not followed even for a single month. In the end, there was no leader who was willing to raise levies, but each fled as quickly as he could; nor even in the end would one shire [county] help another.

In August 1013, Sweyn landed and marched throughout England. Ethelred sent his wife, Emma, and his sons Edward and Alfred to Normandy to take refuge with Emma's brother, Duke Richard II. By Christmas Ethelred was forced to flee to the Isle of Wight off the south coast and from there joined Emma in Normandy.

The Danish conquest of England was complete, but Sweyn did not live to enjoy it. He died on February 3, 1014. His son Canute was chosen to succeed him. Canute ruled from 1017 to 1035, and these were years of peace such as England had not known since the days of Athelstan a century earlier. Canute was a wise and just king. He enacted a set of laws and decreed that the English and the Danes should be equal and live in peace. Although he had a mistress, Algifu, and a son by her, Harold Harefoot, he sought to link himself to the old royal family by recalling Emma from Normandy in 1017 and marrying her, Ethelred having died in 1016. They had one son, Hardecanute.

One Englishman who rose to power under Canute was Godwin. No one knows his background, but whatever his origins, Godwin soon became one of the most powerful men in the kingdom. While still in his twenties he was Canute's closest adviser. He was made earl of Wessex and ran the country when Canute was away in Denmark. He also was the father of Harold, who later became King Harold II.

Canute's Successors

In 1035 Canute died. His dying wish was that his throne go to Hardecanute, his son by Emma. Hardecanute, however, was in Denmark and could not leave because of a threatened invasion from Norway. An assembly of English nobles in Oxford elected Harold Harefoot, Canute's son by Algifu, to be regent, ruling in Hardecanute's place. Two years later Harold Harefoot was recognized as king.

Canute Orders the Tide to Stop

King Canute, who ruled England in addition to Denmark, was considered a wise and just monarch. He realized that his powers, even as a king, were limited and on one occasion demonstrated this to his followers, according to this story, written by Henry of Huntingdon centuries later:

When at the summit of his power [Canute] ordered a seat to be placed for him on the sea-shore when the tide was coming in; thus seated, he shouted to the flowing sea, "Thou, too, art subject to my command, as the land on which I am seated is mine; and no one has ever resisted my commands with impunity [freedom from punishment]. I command you, then, not to flow over my land, nor presume to wet the feet and the robe of your lord."

The tide, however, continued to rise as usual, dashed over his feet and legs without respect to his royal person. Then the King leapt backwards, saying "Let all men know how empty and worthless is the power of kings, for there is none worthy of the name, but He whom heaven, earth, and sea obey by eternal laws."

From henceforth King Canute never wore his crown of gold, but placed it for a lasting memorial on the image of Our Lord affixed to a cross, to the honour of God the almighty King: through whose mercy may the soul of Canute, the King, enjoy everlasting rest.

King Canute, son of King Sweyn, was thought to be a wise ruler. Under his rule, England remained at peace.

In 1036 Alfred, son of Emma and Ethelred and half brother of Hardecanute and Harold Harefoot, sailed from Normandy to England. His announced purpose was to visit his mother, but one account says that six hundred troops accompanied him. Perhaps fearing an uprising, Godwin, acting on behalf of Harold Harefoot, intercepted Alfred. Godwin ordered Alfred's followers to be killed, blinded, or sold into slavery. Alfred was taken aboard a ship and blinded and mutilated so savagely that he died soon afterward. This brutal deed shocked the people of the time and was a permanent stain on Godwin's character. It also earned him the undying hatred of Alfred's brother Edward.

Harold Harefoot died in 1040, and Hardecanute became king. He ordered Godwin to stand trial for the murder of Alfred, but Godwin protested that all he had done was at Harold Harefoot's command. Godwin presented Hardecanute with a splendid gift—a warship complete with eighty handpicked warriors—and was forgiven.

Hardecanute reigned only two years. He was only twenty-five when, at a wedding feast, "standing at his drink, he suddenly fell to the ground with fearful convulsions, and those who were near caught him, and he spoke no word afterwards." Edward, called the Confessor, was elected king, and the royal line of Alfred the Great was restored.

The Young William

Meanwhile, across the English Channel, Duke Robert I of Normandy had died in 1035 while on a pilgrimage. He left as his heir a seven-year-old, illegitimate son, William, known to the rest of France as William the Bastard. Over the next thirty years William not only survived attacks from both within and without his duchy, but he also became one of the strongest rulers in Europe—strong enough to invade England and earn a new nickname, the Conqueror.

Sometime early in 1027 Duke Robert, known as Robert the Devil for his cruelty in war, had been attracted by a girl named Herléve in the town of Falaise in northwestern France. Herléve, the daughter of a leather tanner, was, according to various stories, either dancing in the street or washing linen in a stream when he first saw her. Robert made her his mistress, and she bore their son, William, in either 1027 or 1028. Then in 1034 Robert astounded everyone by announcing that he would make a pilgrimage to Jerusalem. His nobles tried to discourage him, but his mind was made up.

Robert called the leading men of Normandy together and made them swear loyalty to his son, William. He convinced the king of France, Henry I, whom he had recently aided, to recognize William as Robert's heir. Shortly afterward Robert left Normandy, never to return. He reached Jerusalem but died on the return trip.

William the Conqueror inherited the Normandy throne at age seven. It was only by being protected from harm as a child that William was allowed to grow up and become a great warrior and king.

For two years after the seven-year-old William inherited Normandy, the duchy was quiet, held together by his great-uncle, Archbishop Robert of Rouen. When Robert died in 1037, Normandy almost fell apart. The civil war that raged for ten years was not by one side against another; rather, it was everyone for himself. The leading nobles battled one another, and the prize was William.

Some wanted to kill the young duke and replace him. Others wanted to control him. To be close to William was to invite death. William's uncle Walter, Herléve's brother, slept close to his nephew and frequently fled with him from the castle at night to spend the night in a peasant's cottage.

The Battle of Val-és-Dunes

In 1046 a more organized rebellion took shape under William's cousin, Guy of Burgundy. The rebels planned to seize William, but he was warned ahead of time and, by riding all night, escaped and fled to Henry I of France to ask for help. The king considered Guy too much of a threat. He came to William's aid

The Development of Armor

Throughout the history of warfare, as weapons improved, so did the armor worn by soldiers to protect themselves from the weapons. From Roman times through the Battle of Hastings, the chief weapon was the sword. It was not the long, slim piercing blade of later centuries, but shorter, broader, and used for hacking and slashing.

The common form of armor in the Roman legions was the cuirass, or breastplate. Most common soldiers wore cuirasses of padded leather to deflect sword strokes, although some featured thin plates of metal held together with leather thongs. Their officers might have breastplates of metal, sometimes highly ornamented.

Leather caps, sometimes reinforced with metal, were worn by Roman legionnaires to protect their heads. The officers wore metal helmets, often with feathers or plumes on top.

By the time of the Battle of Hastings, more protection was needed than was provided by leather, not only from swords, but also from axes, spears, and arrows. The people of northern Europe—including the English, Normans, and Danes—did not have the skill to make plates of metal armor. Instead they used chain mail, interlinking rings of iron sewn onto their leather tunics.

As a rule only the nobles could afford chain mail, although common soldiers sometimes stripped coats from slain enemies. It had an advantage, even over the old Roman metal armor, in that it was supple and gave the wearer freedom of movement.

In later centuries bows and arrows were perfected to the point where they could easily penetrate chain mail. As a result, heavy metal-plate armor was developed, the type commonly associated with the legendary knights of the Round Table.

Eventually with the development of guns, no armor, however thick, provided enough protection. It was not until the development of new materials in our own century that body armor, such as bulletproof vests, came to be worn again.

A warrior in full armor is received by a king. The development of chain mail gave the soldier protection from weapons without inhibiting his freedom of movement.

and defeated Guy at the battle of Val-és-Dunes in 1047. William, now about twenty, distinguished himself by killing several of the enemy in hand-to-hand fighting.

Three years later a new foe, Geoffrey Martel, count of Anjou, conquered le Maine and threatened Normandy from the south. William now first demonstrated his military genius and ferocity. He moved swiftly against Geoffrey's stronghold of Alençon, taking it by surprise. He captured the town outside the castle and, taking thirty-two prisoners, had their hands and feet cut off and thrown over the castle walls. The castle quickly surrendered, fearful of suffering the same brutality. William was often to use this strategy of deliberate cruelty as an example to others, in both Normandy and England.

William now had not only survived, but had grown so powerful that King Henry was growing nervous. In 1054, the French king joined forces with Geoffrey and planned a two-pronged attack against Normandy. Henry would lead an army from the west and his half brother, Odo, another army from the east.

King Henry I of France (pictured) aided Duke William of Normandy in subduing rebelling nobles, but later, as William became more powerful, engaged in a war against William and was defeated.

The Truce of God

Warfare was almost a constant aspect of French life in the tenth and eleventh centuries. Kings, dukes, and counts fought against one another in ever shifting alliances. The losers in every case were the peasants, whose homes and farms were often destroyed by armies of both sides.

The church probably knew it could not stop the fighting altogether, but it at least tried to limit it by invoking the Truce of God. Under the truce, private warfare was prohibited from Wednesday evening until Monday morning and during the religious seasons of Advent, Lent, Easter, and Pentecost. Those breaking the Truce of God could be excommunicated, or cut off, by the church, and be unable to receive sacraments such as baptism, communion, or marriage.

The church tried to impose the Truce of God in Normandy in 1041 to stop some of the disorder that had broken out after William the Conqueror's father died, but the warring nobles refused to accept it. After William's victory at Val-és-Dunes in 1047, the Truce of God was imposed. It was significant, and a source of strength to William, that he was personally exempted from the truce. The church evidently recognized the need for a strong ruler with the ability to put down rebellions.

Odo's army entered eastern Normandy, making the little town of Mortemer its headquarters. The French grew so careless that they were totally unprepared when William's troops, led by Roger of Mortemer, attacked and defeated them. William was with another part of his army facing King Henry in the west. When he heard the news from Mortemer, he sent a messenger to slip into the French camp and startle them from their sleep by shouting, "Frenchmen, Frenchmen! Arise, arise! You sleep too much. . . . Go bury your friends, who have died in Mortemer." Henry lost his nerve and hastily retreated from Normandy.

William in Control

The Battle of Mortemer was the end of William's fight for survival. He had unified Normandy and had gained control of Ponthieu to the north and le Maine to the south. Henry tried once more to control his too-powerful duke. He invaded Normandy in 1057 and was defeated by William at the Battle of Varaville. Henry was never to set foot in Normandy again. He died in 1060, as did his ally, Geoffrey Martel, and William was at last secure.

William's position was strengthened by the fact that the new king of France, Philip I, was a child whose guardian was Count Baldwin of Flanders, an independent state north of France. In 1051, William had married Matilda, Baldwin's daughter. Therefore, thanks to his father-in-law's influence, William had little to fear from the young king of France.

In England, meanwhile, King Edward had had a difficult reign. He was a quiet, studious man of thirty-seven when he became king in 1042. He was extremely religious, so much so that he was called Edward the Confessor. He had been raised in the Norman court and much preferred the French speech and customs to those of his English subjects. Politically he was completely under the thumb of Godwin of Wessex. In 1045 Edward married—probably against his will—Godwin's daughter Edith.

In 1051, the same year as William's marriage to Matilda, a series of events began that was to have great impact on the futures of Normandy and England. First was the temporary fall from power of Godwin. A Norman noble, Eustace of Boulogne, had been on a visit to the English court of Edward. On his return trip Eustace stopped in Dover and demanded lodging and food for himself and his party. A fight broke out between the townspeople and Eustace's followers, and several Normans were killed.

Eustace complained to Edward, who ordered Godwin, in whose earldom Dover lay, to discipline the city. Godwin, jealous of his king's Norman companions, refused and instead demanded that Eustace's men be handed over for punishment. Edward, in one of his rare shows of strength, accused Godwin of treason and, furthermore, of the murder of Edward's brother Alfred years before.

King Edward the Confessor, quiet and studious, later defeated Godwin to decisively remain on the throne of England. Unfortunately, Edward's favoritism toward Normans would sow the seeds of his later demise.

Godwin in Revolt

Godwin answered by gathering an army from his own earldom and those of his sons. Two other powerful earls, however—Siward of Northumbria and Leofric of Mercia—supported Edward, no doubt jealous of Godwin's power. Moreover, Edward took the step of calling out the national militia—in theory, every able-bodied man in the kingdom. Now, even some of Godwin's men deserted him.

Godwin, seeing he was beaten, tried to make peace, but Edward now had the advantage and used it to gain his revenge. He deprived Godwin and his sons of their earldoms and exiled them from England. He shut up his queen, Godwin's daughter Edith, in a nunnery.

Finally free of Godwin's domination, the king fully demonstrated his preference for Normans. Robert of Jumiéges, the Norman bishop of London, was made archbishop of Canterbury, head of the English church. Norman nobles, including Eustace of Boulogne, were given estates, many of which had been stripped from Godwin and his sons.

William's Queen

The wedding of William of Normandy and Matilda of Flanders that took place in 1051 had been arranged two years earlier. For some reason, however, the church had prohibited the marriage.

One story, since proven false, was that Matilda was already married. Another version was that Matilda, like William, was descended from Rolf and they were too closely related to marry. Yet another said that the union was banned because of a marriage contracted, but never made, between William's uncle and Matilda's mother.

The real reason was probably political. The pope, Leo IX, was a cousin and ally of the German emperor Henry III. Matilda's father, Count Baldwin of Flanders, was an enemy of the emperor. The pope, therefore, likely prohibited the marriage to try to deprive Baldwin of a powerful ally.

When the marriage took place in spite of the ban, William was excommunicated, or cut off from the church, and Normandy placed under an interdict, which meant that no church services could take place. Some sort of agreement was quickly reached, but it was not until 1059 that the marriage was sanctioned, and then only after William and Matilda promised to build two large abbeys.

Matilda was a great help to her husband, ruling Normandy while he was in England. For his part, William apparently was faithful to Matilda all their married life—a rarity among kings in those days—and mourned her greatly when she died in 1083. She and William had four sons and at least five daughters.

Matilda was said to be very beautiful and very small. Indeed, when her tomb at Caen in Normandy was later opened, the bones were those of a woman who could not have been much more than four feet tall.

Shortly thereafter there occurred a key event in English history. Edward named William of Normandy heir to the throne of England. There is no record of what kind of relationship had existed between Edward and William during the years Edward spent in Normandy. Evidently, however, Edward thought highly of his cousin. Also, William's victory at Val-és-Dunes and his marriage to the count of Flanders's daughter may have convinced Edward that here was an heir more worthy than any in England.

Edward continued to shower favors on Normans and bring them into England in ever-increasing numbers. This became too much for the English, who had no more love for the Normans than did Godwin. The mood of the country turned against Edward. The banished Godwin, who had sought refuge in Ireland, gathered a small fleet and sailed back to England, landing at several points along the southern coast. At each point he was hailed as a hero and deliverer, or rescuer, and gathered more ships and men. The king's Norman friends, seeing the way things were going, fled. Robert of Jumiéges had to fight his way out of London.

Godwin in Triumph

Deserted, Edward was forced to give in. Godwin did not have long to enjoy his triumph, however, for he suffered a fatal stroke while dining with Edward in 1053. Since his oldest son, Sweyn, had been outlawed and banished in 1048 for kidnapping a nun, Godwin's next son, Harold, took his place. Harold's position was strengthened when Siward, earl of Northumbria, died in 1057, and the earldom went to Harold's younger brother, Tostig.

The most dramatic, and in many ways the most controversial, event leading up to the Battle of Hastings occurred in 1064. Harold, now the most powerful man in England, wound up a virtual prisoner of William of Normandy. Records of the episode exist not only in chronicles, but also in pictures, something extremely rare for this period. These pictures of the Norman Conquest are contained in the Bayeux Tapestry, a strip of linen 230 feet long and 20 inches wide.

According to the tapestry, Edward sent Harold on a mission to Normandy, perhaps to confirm Edward's promise that William should succeed him. This seems unlikely. Even if Harold had received such orders, he would not have wanted to put himself at the mercy of a possible enemy and was strong enough to refuse. More probable is the version that Harold was not headed to Normandy at all, but to some unknown destination when he was shipwrecked on the coast of France in Ponthieu, whose count delivered him to William.

William took advantage of the situation. Harold was allowed to return to England only after he swore an oath to William. What the oath was or why he swore it has been debated for centuries. Most historians believe that Harold promised to support William as King Edward's heir, but did he do so freely? Some say he did, thinking he would be William's counselor just as he was Edward's. Others say he did not, fearing that his place would be taken by William's Norman advisers. Still others say he took the oath only to win his freedom, expecting to go back on his word later.

The Bayeux Tapestry shows the scene in great detail. William, seated on his throne, points a finger at Harold, who stands with one hand on an altar and one on a chest. A story grew up later that William had tricked Harold, concealing holy relics, such as the bones of saints, in the chest and that Harold was dismayed to discover he had taken a much stronger oath than he thought. While no English writers of the time mentioned Harold's journey or oath,

A scene from the Bayeux Tapestry shows Harold touching two shrines and taking an oath of allegiance to William before returning to England.

the Norman chroniclers gave it great emphasis. This was natural, considering that the breaking of the oath would be one of William's chief justifications for invading England.

William's climb had been much like that of the duchy of Normandy itself—both came a long way in a short time. In only 150 years, a band of pirates had formed one of the strongest states in Europe. And, demonstrating the same kind of energy as his Viking forebears, William had gone from being a hunted youth to a powerful duke. Two years later he would attempt the greatest leap of all—to the throne of England.

CHAPTER THREE

Prelude to War

King Edward the Confessor died on January 5, 1066. He had been too ill eight days earlier even to attend the consecration on the Isle of Thorney west of London of his rebuilt and expanded Saint Peter's Church, better known as Westminster Abbey. He left no children, and his death began a three-way struggle for the throne of England that was to end with the Battle of Hastings.

As he lay dying, Edward summoned the leading men of the kingdom. Queen Edith sat at the foot of his bed, warming his feet. Edward stretched out his hand to Harold and said:

> This woman [Edith] and all the kingdom I commend to your charge. . . . I also commend to you those men who have left their native land [his Norman friends] for love of me, and who have served me loyally. Accept their fealty [allegiance] if they wish to give it . . . or if not, send them under your protection to their homes.

Harold took this to mean that Edward wished him to become king, and he wasted no time making the wish come true. The next day, just hours after Edward was buried in his new abbey, Harold was hurriedly elected by an assembly of nobles and became the first king of England to be crowned there. The *Anglo-Saxon Chronicle* said he "was not to enjoy a tranquil reign while he ruled the kingdom." He knew that he would likely have to fight for his throne.

Harold was forty-three years old when he became king. He was tall, handsome, and regarded as a just and wise man. He

In a drawing that depicts the Bayeux Tapestry, Harold is crowned king of England in Westminster Abbey. In having himself crowned, Harold acted in direct opposition to his pledge of allegiance to William.

was a strong ruler, and "disturbers of the peace, thieves and robbers, this champion of the law threatened with the terrible face of a lion."

Nevertheless, he was under a cloud from the moment he took the throne. For one thing, he was not a member of the royal family and was looked on by some as an upstart son of an upstart father—Godwin. For another, there was the extreme haste of his coronation. Many of the leading men of the north and west had not had time to come to London. A new king had been elected before they knew the old king was dead. Some people muttered that Harold, earl of Wessex, had been elected king by an assembly dominated by his own subjects.

An Unpleasant Surprise

Edward's death and Harold's coronation was also a shock, and a very unpleasant one, in Normandy. Supposedly, Duke William was hunting outside the city of Rouen when he heard the news. He handed his bow to a servant and spoke to no one. The only outward sign of his inner feeling was a repeated lacing and unlacing of his cloak. Still silent, he rode back to the castle, drew his cloak over his face, and sat against a pillar, deep in thought. For fifteen years, ever since he had been named by Edward as his successor, he had expected to be the next king of England. Now, someone else—someone who only two years earlier had sworn an oath to uphold William's claim—was on the throne.

When his closest friend, William Fitzosbern, finally dared approach him, he rose, determined to take England by force. In truth, he had little choice. All Normandy knew of Edward's promise to William in 1051 and of Harold's oath in 1064. If William declined to assert his claim, he would lose face in his own duchy and throughout Europe.

Westminster Abbey

When King Edward the Confessor was forced to accept Godwin of Wessex back from exile in 1052, he began to turn more and more away from governing England and toward religious works. The most important of these was the building of Westminster Abbey.

The site was the Isle of Thorney, west of London, a bramble-covered piece of ground surrounded by the Thames and Tyburn Rivers. According to legend the first church on the island had been founded by Saberht, first Christian king of the east Saxons. It was dedicated to Saint Peter, and the saint himself was supposed to have appeared personally to consecrate it.

With Godwin running his kingdom, Edward made the rebuilding of Saint Peter's Church his life's work. It had begun in 1050, and Edward was determined to make it the largest, finest church in England.

The church was designed on the Norman pattern, in the shape of a cross, with a main tower and two lesser towers. As it grew, it came to be known by the people as West Minster, as opposed to the East Minster, Saint Paul's Cathedral in London.

When Saint Peter's Church was dedicated on November 28, 1065, Edward was too ill to attend and died a week later. His successor, Harold, became the first English king to be crowned at Westminster. William the Conqueror was also crowned there as has been every monarch since.

A shrine to Edward remains at Westminster, but the original building has all but disappeared. It was rebuilt, mostly by William's great-great-great-grandson, Henry III, two hundred years later.

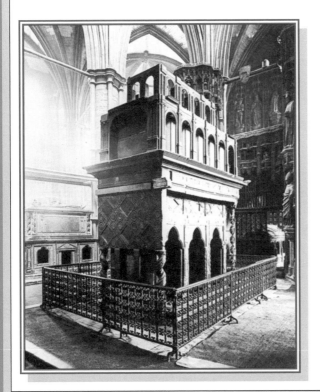

The shrine of Edward the Confessor in Westminster Abbey.

Immediately William sent a message to Harold. Its contents are not known, but it probably was a reminder of Harold's oath and a demand that Harold relinquish the throne to William. William was realistic enough to know that the message would have no effect, and it did not. Harold replied that he had been chosen king by the leading men of England, anointed by the church, and would defend his title. William's formal request had been denied. The only means left to him was invasion.

A full-scale invasion of England was an awesome challenge. Defending his duchy and attacking his neighbors was one thing. The conquest of so large a kingdom as England, especially as it involved crossing the English Channel, was quite another. Both the Anglo-Saxon and Danish invasions had been drawn out over centuries, and neither required the transporting of horses. Only the mighty Roman Empire had ever succeeded in such a venture.

William knew he would need the solid support of Normandy, but that proved difficult to obtain. Although descended from sea-going Vikings, the Norman counts were landsmen and hesitated to embark on a foreign adventure. Their oaths to William bound them to fight for him to defend Normandy or against a hostile neighbor but said nothing about crossing the channel to invade England.

The Lillebonne Conference

In February 1066 William called his nobles together at Lillebonne in Normandy. His object was to explain to them his reasons for wanting to invade England and to gain their support. Somewhat to William's surprise, the nobles were doubtful about an overseas venture. They wanted some time to talk about his ambitious plan.

William Fitzosbern listened to his fellow nobles and seemed to agree with them that the venture was not worth the risk. Knowing how close he was to the duke, the nobles elected Fitzosbern to speak for them.

When the assembly reconvened and Fitzosbern rose to speak, however, he praised the planned invasion. Turning to his comrades, he said:

> What are you waiting for? He is your master and requires your services. It is your duty to come forward with a good heart and honour your obligations. Fail him in this and it will be the worse for you in the end. Now is the time to prove your loyalty.

Turning to Duke William, Fitzosbern then pledged not only his loyalty and support, but also that of every man in the room. The strategy did not work. There were angry shouts from throughout the room, and the meeting broke up in confusion.

William changed his strategy and called his nobles in one by

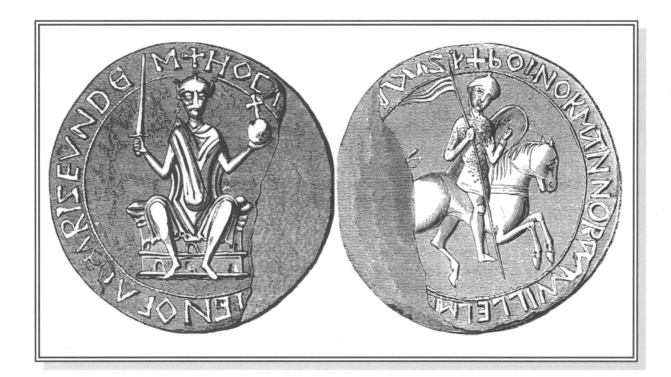

one. It was one thing to say no to William in a group, but quite another in person. Each man was persuaded not only to support the invasion, but to agree to furnish a specific number of ships or fighting men. The clever William had a scribe on hand to write down each bargain in case any of the nobles had faulty memories afterward.

Normandy, powerful though it was, would be no match for the number of troops Harold could muster. William needed allies, and from the most important one he needed not soldiers, but a blessing. Archdeacon Gilbert of Lisieux was sent to Rome to convince the Catholic Church to support William, arguing that Harold had broken a sacred vow.

The quarrel between William and Harold now reached a new level. For hundreds of years the English church had tended to depart from the rules set down by the popes in Rome. For instance, most of its business was conducted in English rather than in Latin. Pope Alexander II, encouraged by the influential Cardinal Hildebrand, who later became the reformer Pope Gregory VII, saw William's plea as a chance to gain control over the church in England.

The seal of William the Conqueror is etched with his image.

The Pope's Blessing

The church also was trying to gain more influence over nonreligious affairs in Europe. Only recently, as a result of Hildebrand's efforts, had the church won the right to elect its own popes,

The Bayeux Tapestry

The most famous account of the Norman Conquest is not a written record, but a pictorial one. The Bayeux Tapestry, eight sections totaling 230 feet in length, tells the story from Harold of Wessex's visit to William of Normandy through the Battle of Hastings.

Actually the Bayeux Tapestry is not a tapestry at all. A true tapestry is a cloth woven on a loom, using different colors of thread to form a picture. The Bayeux Tapestry is embroidery, consisting of pieces of linen with pictures sewed on in colored thread.

Originally it was thought to have been made, or at least ordered made, by William's wife, Matilda. In fact, it was commissioned by William's half brother, Bishop Odo of Bayeux, who is given a prominent role in the pictures. It was probably made in England by English needleworkers since some of the place-names and spellings are unmistakably Anglo-Saxon.

The Bayeux Tapestry was made between 1070 and 1080 and kept at Bayeux Cathedral in Normandy over the centuries as one of its greatest treasures. It was almost destroyed during the French Revolution in 1789 but survived and was later taken to Paris and exhibited at the order of Napoleon Bonaparte, who was planning an invasion of England.

It was returned to Bayeux and, during the German occupation of France in World War II, was studied by Adolf Hitler's generals, who also were planning to invade England. It was cleaned and restored in 1983 and now is displayed in the Center of William the Conqueror near the Bayeux Cathedral.

The Bayeux Tapestry depicts the events of the Norman Conquest of England.

instead of having them named by kings. Here was a chance to establish the church as the judge of disputes over who should be king. Alexander II agreed to give William's invasion his blessing, thus turning it into something of a religious crusade. Gilbert returned to Normandy with a papal banner for William to carry and a relic, said to be a bone, from Saint Peter to wear into battle.

Now it was much easier for William to gain allies. Nobles and soldiers volunteered from throughout France. The enterprise had taken on the air of a crusade instead of naked aggression. William's allies could tell themselves they were doing God's will, even if there was plunder in it for them, as well.

The forests along the Norman coast now began to ring with the sound of axes as trees were chopped down for shipbuilding. The Bayeux Tapestry shows carpenters hard at work with their tools and dragging the finished ships to the sea. Chronicler William of Jumiéges estimated the number of ships at 3,000, but only about 780 had been promised, and probably not all these were built. Another writer, Wace, said that his father, who fought at Hastings, told him there were 696 vessels. These were not ships in the modern sense, but more like open boats, most of them far smaller than Viking ships and nowhere near as advanced in construction.

While the shipbuilding continued, William gathered supplies, not for the journey to England—that would take only a single day—but to keep his troops fed until it was time to sail. He was so organized and successful that the soldiers did not simply take what they wanted from the surrounding countryside. The duke's chaplain, William of Poitiers, wrote that he "made generous provision both for his own knights and for those from other parts, but he did not allow any of them to take their sustenance [food] by force. . . . A weak and unarmed man might watch the swarm of soldiers without fear."

In this scene from the Bayeux Tapestry, men cut down trees in the forests along the Norman coast to build ships in preparation for a Norman invasion of Britain.

Harold Prepares for War

In England, meanwhile, Harold was not idle. He was aware of William's preparations and made ready to meet the invasion. A sense of urgency was in the air. In April a "fiery dragon" appeared in the night sky. It was Halley's comet, which appears every eighty-six years, but to the people of the time it was a sign of momentous events to come.

In June Harold called up his army and prepared his fleet. The fleet was not intended to intercept William's

King Edward's Vision

As Edward the Confessor lay dying, he had a vision that he relayed to those gathered around his bed. The vision was that his kingdom would be destroyed.

He said that two monks he had known in his youth, now long dead, appeared to him and said that because of the wickedness of the nobles and high clergy in England, "God has given this kingdom, within a year and a day of your death, under His curse into the hands of enemies, and fiends shall pass through the whole land and harry [destroy] it with fire and sword."

Edward said he asked the monks when the kingdom would be restored, and they answered, "In that time when a green tree, cut down in the middle of its trunk and carried three furlongs [about 660 yards] from its roots, shall be joined again to the trunk without the help of man and begin once more to put forth fresh leaves."

After William the Conqueror's victory at Hastings, this vision was often debated. Centuries later it was said that the rejoined "green tree" symbolized King Henry II, the first ruler of England descended from both William the Conqueror and, through his grandmother, Alfred the Great.

In a rendition of the Bayeux Tapestry, Harold and his men point to Halley's comet, taken as a portent of momentous events.

ships. The ships of the time were incapable of such precise sailing. They were unwieldy and had only a single mast with one square sail, good only when the wind was at their back. Instead, ships were used to transport armies. Harold hoped to be able to rely on soldiers to keep William's army busy wherever it landed until a larger army sailed or rowed to help out.

The English army was made up of three types of soldiers. First were the housecarls, Harold's personal corps of hand-picked men. This body of professional soldiers had been introduced in England by Canute. They numbered only about four thousand, but they were perhaps the finest fighters in Europe. Next came the two groups making up the *fyrd*, or militia. The so-called select *fyrd* consisted of the minor nobles known as thegns, or thanes, and men recruited from their individual areas. Every five hides, units of land whose sizes varied widely throughout the country, were supposed to furnish one soldier. When mustered, the *fyrd*'s term of service was supposed to be limited to sixty days. Last was the great *fyrd*, consisting of every able-bodied man in the kingdom who might be called on to fight in a national emergency. Poorly organized and armed, their purpose was to lend sheer numbers to the better-equipped force.

Harold put the housecarls and some of the select *fyrd*, about twelve thousand men in all, along the southern coast facing Normandy. There they waited to repel the invasion they knew was sure to come. They waited and waited, gazing week after week into an empty sea, but no enemy appeared.

It was not that William did not want to invade. He was unable to. His army was gathered, and his fleet was finally assembled by August at the mouth of the River Dives, but it was unable to go anywhere. A south wind was needed before the unwieldy ships could sail north for England. All through August the wind blew steadily from the north, while William fumed and fretted onshore. It is a tribute to his leadership that he was able to hold together his army, many of whom were volunteers or paid mercenaries.

The *Fyrd* Is Dismissed

In England Harold had similar problems. There is no task more boring for a soldier than guard duty, and his army was growing restless. Supplies were getting low. The soldiers' sixty days of duty had long since been fulfilled. They missed their families. Most of them were not professional soldiers, but farmers, and the time for harvesting hay was at hand. Harold gambled that William had missed his chance, that the normal north winds and rough waters of the English Channel in September would make sailing impossible. On September 8 he withdrew the housecarls, dismissed the *fyrd*, and ordered the fleet back to London. On the way a storm struck, and many ships were lost.

On September 12 the wind changed to the west, and William sailed. Some experts think he intended to invade England; others, that he simply wanted to move his fleet to a port closer to England. Either way, the same storm that struck Harold's fleet also hit the Normans, driving them east to Saint Valéry on the Somme River in Ponthieu, whose count was loyal to William. A few ships were wrecked, and William had the dead buried secretly so that the rest of his troops would not lose courage. He readied the fleet and waited once more for a favorable wind. He was now only a little more than fifty miles from England instead of a hundred.

Harold was probably not too worried about his lost ships. The channel storm had reinforced his opinion that weather would prevent any invasion from Normandy until at least the next year. No sooner had he settled down in London, however, than he received astonishing news. Harald Hardraade of Norway had landed in the north with a fleet of three hundred ships.

CHAPTER FOUR

The Battles in the North

The Battle of Hastings is one of the best known in world history. Its outcome might have been far different, however, had it not been for two earlier and often overlooked clashes—the Battles of Fulford Gate and Stamford Bridge. These battles marked the end of more than 250 years of Scandinavian invasions of England, but the victorious English were weakened to the point that it may have made William's triumph at Hastings possible.

William and Harold were not the only claimants for the crown of England in 1066. The third contender was Harald Hardraade, the nickname meaning ruthless or stubborn, king of Norway, and perhaps the most colorful character connected with the Battle of Hastings.

Harald Hardraade had lived an adventurous life, even by Viking standards. He was fifty years old in 1066, a huge man famous for his ferocity in battle, his cruelty toward enemies, and his iron-fisted rule over his subjects, but also known for his harp playing and poetry.

The son of a minor king named Sigurd, Harald was a warrior from the time he was old enough to wield an ax. When only fifteen, he was wounded while fighting for his half brother, King Olaf of Norway. Olaf was killed, and Harald had to flee to Sweden. When he recovered, he led a band of followers south through Russia to the kingdom of Novgorod, where he served under its king.

After a year or two he made his way farther south to Constantinople, the capital of the Byzantine Empire and one of the world's wealthiest cities. There, the tall, handsome, and dashing Harald caught the eye of Empress Zöe, who enlisted him in her personal guard, and he soon became its captain.

Harald fought for the empress in Sicily and North Africa. He became famous throughout the Mediterranean not only for his fighting ability, but also for his cleverness. Once, unable to take a city by force, he had a rumor spread that he had fallen ill and died. His followers tearfully requested permission to bury their dead leader in the city, but once inside the gates the mourners whipped out their swords and sacked the town.

Escape from Constantinople

Empress Zöe, although an old woman and already married, wanted Harald as a husband. When he preferred her niece, Maria, the empress threw him in prison. According to legend, yet another woman in love with Harald helped him and his followers escape. Harald abducted Maria, fought his way out of the city, and returned to Novgorod to claim the fortune in gold he had sent there for safekeeping.

Harald returned to Norway, where his nephew, King Magnus I, made him co-ruler. He became sole king when Magnus died in 1047. For years afterward he tried to add Denmark to his kingdom but failed. Looking around for someone else to fight, he thought of England, recalling that Magnus and King Hardecanute had made each other their heirs if they died childless. Harald reasoned that Magnus's claim to England was now his, and in 1066 he was convinced to pursue it by Tostig, younger brother of King Harold of England.

A drawing depicts Empress Zöe and her court in Constantinople.

A Cruel People

Life in the Scandinavian countries was harsh and cruel, with bitterly cold winters and months during which there were only a few hours of daylight. It was no wonder that the warriors who descended on Europe from Denmark and Norway were themselves harsh and cruel.

For more than two centuries those who lived along the coasts of England, Ireland, and France lived in dread of the day when long ships adorned by carved dragons' heads emerged from the mist and Viking warriors swarmed ashore. The prospect of being robbed was not all that frightening, for it was a rough age, and thieves and outlaws were not uncommon. What terrified their victims was the Vikings' seeming love of mindless violence. A new prayer, "From the fury of the Northmen, Lord deliver us," was recited in churches.

The Vikings killed for the sake of killing, destroyed for the sake of destruction. When they had taken all the loot their ships could possibly hold, they would set fire to what was left. Not only did they slaughter any who dared oppose them, they also hunted and killed those who fled, including women and children.

They took delight in torturing their victims before they killed them. Their most gruesome practice, one saved for enemies they hated the most, was called the blood eagle. While the unlucky person was still alive, his lungs were pulled from his chest through cuts made along the ribs.

One Viking legend tells how warriors were amusing themselves by tossing children back and forth on the points of their spears. When one warrior, more tenderhearted than the rest, objected, the others taunted him for being a weakling. They gave him the nickname Barna-Karl, or child's friend.

What made the Vikings so feared, in addition to their cruelty, was their absolute fearlessness in battle. This stemmed from their religion, the worship of a warlike collection of gods such as Odin and Thor. The Vikings believed that the time of each person's death was ordained by the gods and that nothing could be done to change that destiny. As a result they had no fear in battle, reasoning that death could be neither avoided nor sought.

For two centuries, the appearance of Vikings along the coast of Europe sent dread into the hearts of the inhabitants. The Vikings' mindless cruelty surprised and appalled those who encountered them.

Tostig had been made earl of Northumberland in 1055. He proved such a harsh ruler that his people revolted in 1065. To keep the peace, King Edward, with the support of Tostig's brother Harold, had the Northumbrian earl outlawed and exiled. After Edward's death Tostig wanted revenge. He first approached King Sweyn of Denmark about invading England but was turned down.

He next tried his luck in Norway, first trying to get Harald Hardraade to help him win the throne. Harald answered that the Norsemen would not be eager to fight to help the Englishman. Besides, he said, "men say that Englishmen are not to be trusted."

Tostig then changed tactics, offering to help Harald win the English crown. Tostig said:

> I am as good as my brother, except for the fact that I am not king. Everyone knows that no such a fighting man as you has ever been born in the north. If you wish to conquer England then I can arrange that many of [England's] lords will be your friends and supporters, for I lack nothing against my brother save the title of king. . . . All England lies at your hand.

This was just what Harald wanted to hear, and he began making plans for an invasion.

Their plans were completed in August 1066. By that time the same, persistent north wind that had frustrated William of Normandy was blowing fair for Harald of Norway. His fleet left Norway and sailed to the friendly kingdom of the Shetland and Orkney Islands north of Britain. There he picked up additional ships and men and proceeded to Scotland, meeting Tostig, who had sailed a fleet of ships up the English coast, testing his brother's defenses. After adding still more ships, Harald moved on to England, landing near the town of Scarborough and burning it before going down the coast. His fleet sailed far up the Humber River, landing on September 19 at the village of Riccal. The Vikings scrambled ashore, put on their armor, and set out for their goal, the city of York, only twelve miles away.

The English Reaction

England's two northern earls—Morcar of Northumbria and Edwin of Mercia—had heard about the burning of Scarborough and were in York with all the troops they could gather. On September 20 they marched from the gates of York and met Harald and Tostig at Fulford Gate, about a mile away.

Harald's army advanced along a strip of dry land between the eastern bank of the River Ouse and a watery marsh. The army was in two wings, the stronger next to the riverbank, the weaker next to the marsh. When the Norsemen saw the approaching English, they halted, waiting for an attack.

At first the English were successful. They pushed the weaker Norse wing back, threatening to break through. Then Harald sounded a charge and unfurled his personal banner, called Land Waster—a black raven (a symbol of death) on a white background. The Norsemen advanced in a fury.

They probably used a *svin-fylking* or "swine formation." This popular tactic featured an attacking force shaped like an arrow. At the tip were a few of the bravest and mightiest warriors. Behind them, in an ever wider formation, came the rest of the army. The object was to pierce the enemy lines by brute force.

In all likelihood King Harald himself was at the tip of the arrow, swinging his huge, two-handed ax and screaming with a mindless fury. A warrior who went into battle in such a state of madness was known as a *berserkr*, from which comes the English word *berserk*.

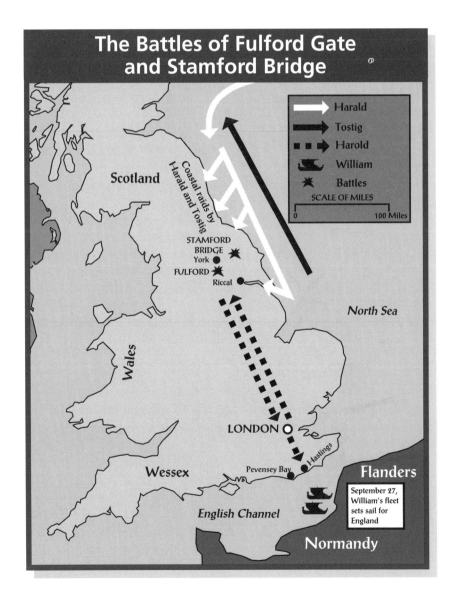

The Battles of Fulford Gate and Stamford Bridge

Harald

Tostig

Harold

William

Battles

SCALE OF MILES

0   100 Miles

Scotland

Coastal raids by Harald and Tostig

STAMFORD BRIDGE

York

FULFORD

Riccal

North Sea

Wales

LONDON

Wessex

Pevensey Bay

Hastings

Flanders

September 27, William's fleet sets sail for England

English Channel

Normandy

The English could not withstand the charge. They were pushed back into the marsh, which was soon so choked with bodies that "the war-keen Norsemen could cross on corpses only." The survivors retreated to York and tried to rally but were overtaken and slaughtered. Edwin and Morcar escaped, but they had lost many men—men who might have been able to fight later at Hastings.

York surrendered, and the victorious Harald and Tostig entered the city. They demanded that one hundred hostages be delivered to them, as a token of the surrender, on September 25 at Stamford Bridge, seven miles east of York. Then they returned in celebration to the fleet at Riccal.

England's King Harold had not been idle—far from it. He left London for York on September 19 with his housecarls, gathering troops along the way. The roads were among the best in England, having been built originally by the Romans, and by the morning of September 25 he arrived in York, 190 miles away. Even with the good roads it was a remarkable march, more so since Harold was ill and had difficulty riding. In York he was joined by Morcar, Edwin, and their troops who had survived the Fulford battle.

Tostig and Harald Hardraade, after the victory at Fulford Gate, enter the city of York to celebrate their victory.

Stamford Bridge

So it was that when Harald Hardraade and Tostig reached Stamford Bridge on the twenty-fifth, they received a surprise. They were not anticipating a battle, and many of their warriors had left their coats of chain mail—tunics on which interlocking iron rings had been sewn—on the ships. But instead of the expected hostages, they saw a marching army, looking "like a sheet of ice when the weapons glittered."

Tostig knew it must be his brother Harold and urged Harald Hardraade to retreat to his fleet. The great Viking, however, was

Viking Ships

A major reason for the success of the Viking raiders was the Scandinavians' skill at shipbuilding. By the time Harald Hardraade's fleet descended on England in 1066, Viking ships were among the best in the world—certainly far superior to those used by William of Normandy to cross the English Channel.

There were three principal categories of Viking ships. The first, the *skuta*, was used along the Scandinavian coastline, seldom venturing out to open sea from the rivers and fjords, or inlets. The *skuta* had ten to fifteen oars on each side and would carry from twenty to fifty men. It was small, swift, and more often used as a means of transportation than a warship. *Skuta* is a predecessor of the English words *scoot* and *shoot*.

The *snekkja* was larger, from seventy to one-hundred feet long, with twenty pairs of oars. It would hold as many as one-hundred warriors and was used mainly for raids along the Scandinavian coast, although it was probably the type of ship used by the early raiders of England and France. It was designed so that it could be sailed or rowed up rivers deep into enemy territory.

The large-scale invasions, such as those by Sweyn Forkbeard, Canute, and Harald Hardraade, were made possible by the development of the *skeid*. Most were from 100 to 150 feet long, although Canute's personal ship was said to be more than 200 feet in length, with sixty oars on each side and the ability to carry several hundred soldiers.

The *skeid* was capable of the then amazing sailing speed of more than eleven knots or about twelve miles an hour. They would average one hundred miles a day on overseas voyages, with the crew sleeping on the open deck regardless of the weather.

The swift and well-built ships of the Vikings gave them a distinct and powerful advantage over all other countries of the time.

determined to fight. The battle began with the Norwegian forces divided, the smaller part on the east side of the River Derwent facing the oncoming English. These soldiers began to scramble across a wooden bridge to rejoin the main force.

When most of them were across, a single Viking warrior stood in the middle of the bridge, determined to hold the English off singlehandedly, while his comrades reorganized. According to chronicles, he killed forty Englishmen, and no one could get past him.

Finally an English soldier found a swill tub—a wooden basket used to carry fish—on the riverbank. He got into the tub, floated under the bridge, and was able to spear the mighty Norseman from below through the gaps in the planks of the bridge. As late as the nineteenth century, the people of the village of Stamford Bridge held a feast to commemorate the battle. Part of the menu consisted of pies shaped like swill tubs.

The Brothers Meet

Next came a lull in the battle. King Harold rode forth with only a small escort, presumably under a flag of truce, and asked if his brother, Tostig, was in the invading army. Tostig rode to meet him, and the brothers faced one another. Harold, seeking to hide his identity from the Norsemen, said to Tostig, "Your brother sends you greetings. He offers you peace and all Northumbria for your own—a third of the kingdom rather than no agreement."

"It is a better choice than you gave me last winter," said Tostig, referring to his exile, "but what does King Harald of Norway get for his trouble?"

"Seven feet of English ground," answered Harold, "or, since he is taller than most, as much again if he needs it."

Tostig answered, "Then go and tell King Harold to be ready for battle. Never let it be said among Norsemen that Earl Tostig deserted their king in the face of a fight."

Tostig rode back to Harald Hardraade, who had heard, but not understood, the conversation in English between the brothers. "Who was that man," the king of Norway said. "He spoke well."

Harold and Tostig meet before the Battle of Stamford Bridge. According to legend, Harold spoke of himself in the third person to disguise his identity.

The Battle-Ax

Although the sword was the most common weapon in the Viking arsenal, the battle-ax was the most feared and was the one most closely associated with the Scandinavian warriors. At the Battle of Hastings, William of Normandy's troops had never before faced such a weapon, which was capable of splitting a man in two or sending both horse and rider to the ground in one blow.

The ax was introduced to England by the Danes and became a favorite weapon of the English. They were wielded to great effect by King Harold's housecarls at Hastings. Most were about four feet long and were used with one hand, while the other held a shield. Exceptionally large and strong men, however, often carried six-foot-long, double-bladed axes swung with both hands.

There were two main types of blades. The first flared out gracefully from the helve, or handle, to form a broad, convex edge. The so-called bearded ax featured a blade that was extended sharply downward at the bottom and had a straight edge.

A warrior's ax was a prized possession. The blades were often intricately carved with mystical symbols designed to make the bearer invincible, or unconquerable. The finest axes and swords sometimes were given names by their owners—highly descriptive names such as Leg Biter, War Flame, and Grey Steel.

"That was King Harold," answered Tostig.

"Quite a small man," commented Harald. "But he stood well in his stirrups." And the Norseman made up a verse on the spot:

Forth we go in our lines
Without our armor, against the blue blades.
The helmets glitter: I have no armor.
Our shrouds are down in those ships.

The battle resumed. The English pushed across the Derwent and in desperate hand-to-hand fighting with swords, spears, and battle-axes, broke through the invaders' main line. Enraged, Harald Hardraade "ran out in front of the array [his personal guard] and hewed [cut] down with both hands so that neither helmet nor armour could withstand him, and all who were nearest gave way before him." Thus isolated, he was an easy target and fell with a spear through his throat.

With the king of Norway dead, the king of England once more offered to make peace with his brother. Instead, Tostig picked up Harald's banner, Land Waster, and the battle went on. Finally Tostig was killed, and it appeared, the battle was over. More Norsemen appeared, however—the reserves who had been left with the ships and who had hurriedly been summoned from Riccal.

The Vikings Destroyed

The fighting continued until nearly sundown, but at last virtually the entire invading force was killed. "While the English savagely harried [attacked] their rear, the remaining Norwegians were put to flight," says the *Anglo-Saxon Chronicle*. "Some were drowned, some were burnt to death . . . diversely they perished, until there were few survivors." Apparently some of the Norsemen took refuge in nearby farmhouses or churches, which were set on fire by the English.

The next day Harold allowed the few Norwegian survivors to sail home, provided they promised never again to attack England. Of the three hundred ships that had brought the army southward, only twenty-four were needed to carry back what was left. The age of Viking conquests was over.

The weary, depleted English army returned to York. For most of the next week it rested and healed its wounded. Then on October 1 Harold was at dinner when a messenger from the south arrived, breathless, with the worst of news. William of Normandy had landed in England.

CHAPTER FIVE

Prelude to Battle

William the Conqueror was lucky. There is no other way to explain why the south wind that would take his invasion fleet to southern England blew at the very moment Harold and his army were busy two hundred miles away in the north. In the two weeks before the Battle of Hastings, however, William would show that his eventual victory was due just as much to his skill as a general as to his luck.

Ever since reaching Saint Valéry on the Somme River in mid-August, William had been waiting for the wind to change. Every morning when he emerged from his quarters, he would look eagerly at the weathervane atop the church. Each morning it pointed south, away from England. Finally William had the casket with the bones of Saint Valéry brought from the church and set up in the courtyard. His army knelt in prayer and tossed so many coins as an offering to the saint that the casket was soon covered. A few days later, on September 27, two days after Harold's victory against the Vikings at Stamford Bridge, the prayers were answered. A thunderstorm passed over, and when the skies cleared, the wind was blowing from the south.

The rest of the day was a mad scramble to load provisions, weapons, and horses into the waiting ships. As one chronicler described it, "Some were calling for their knights or their companions but most, forgetful alike of followers, companions, or provisions, were only eager not to be left behind." The loading was completed by late afternoon, and William ordered the ships to sail to the mouth of the harbor and wait. The crossing would take about twelve hours, and William did not want to land ashore in the dark. At last he raised the signal light in the *Mora*, his flagship given to him by his queen, Matilda. The other ships were supposed to follow that light across the channel.

When morning came, however, the *Mora* was alone on the channel. Some of William's men panicked, but the duke calmly ordered the anchor tossed overboard and "just as if he had been at home in his own dining-hall, ate a copious [large] meal, helped down with spiced and honeyed wine and with memorable gaiety of spirit, affirming that the other ships would not be long in coming." Sure enough, within minutes masts "like a thick forest on the sea" appeared. The *Mora,* finest ship in the fleet, had simply outsailed the rest.

The Normans Land in England

About nine o'clock in the morning the Norman fleet came ashore at Pevensey, a port about ten miles west of Hastings. A body of knights scrambled ashore, weapons ready, but no enemy was in sight. One chronicle said that William, alighting from the *Mora*, slipped and fell on the beach. His men murmured that this was a bad omen, but William cried, "See, my lords! By the splendor of God, I have taken possession of England with both hands. It is mine, and what is mine is yours."

No one knows whether William had intended to land at Pevensey or at Hastings, but within two days the entire army had moved from one to the other. Most of the army went by ship, but William and a group of horsemen took the land route around Pevensey Harbor, destroying several small villages in their path. Reaching Hastings, he put up a wooden fort and sought to discover Harold's whereabouts.

A messenger arrived from Robert Fitzwimarc, a Norman who lived in England and was friendly to Harold, telling William that Harold had won a tremendous victory and was headed south with a huge army. The Norman army, Fitzwimarc said, "was no more use than a pack of curs" and should sail home. William, in a reply he knew would find its way back to Harold, said he had no intention of leaving, that he wanted to fight Harold as quickly as possible, and that even though he had sixty thousand men—which he did not—he would have been just as ready to fight if he had only ten thousand—which was close to the real number.

William the Conqueror reviews his troops. William was incredibly lucky that the wind blew favorably for him, allowing him to land his ships unopposed on the coast of Pevensey.

William had told the truth in at least one respect: he wanted a battle as quickly as possible. First, his army had to live off the surrounding territory and ran the risk of running out of food. Second, the longer he allowed Harold to wait, the more troops Harold could gather. Furthermore, he had to get Harold to come to him. If he marched inland to seek a battle, he risked being cut off from his ships and trapped in a hostile country.

He went about drawing Harold to him in a barbaric, but time-honored way—by destroying Harold's towns and slaughtering his people. Later, during William's reign as king of England, a survey was taken of the kingdom. Next to the names of several villages near Hastings was written the single word *wasta*, "wasted."

Harold on the March

Harold, indeed, was on his way south, but it was at the head of a far smaller army than had marched to Stamford Bridge. The housecarls had suffered major losses. Edwin and Morcar, their forces all but gone after two major battles, stayed in the north. On October 5, barely two weeks after he had left London to meet Harald Hardraade, Harold was back.

Once in London, Harold sent out the call throughout the kingdom for the select *fyrd*, his trained militia. He also called together his most trusted lieutenants to discuss what should be

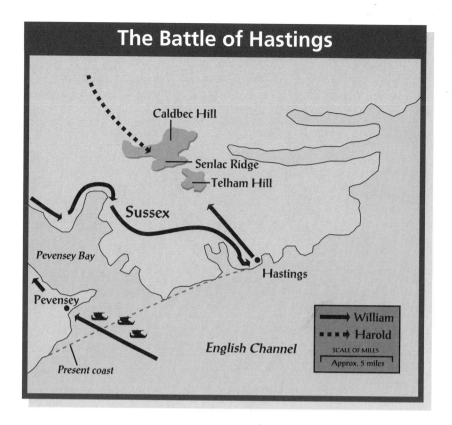

The Battle of Hastings

- Caldbec Hill
- Senlac Ridge
- Telham Hill

Sussex

Pevensey Bay

Hastings

Pevensey

English Channel

Present coast

William
Harold
SCALE OF MILES
Approx. 5 miles

done. His youngest brother, Gyrth, suggested leading the army at once against William. Gyrth argued that Harold was exhausted from his journey, that Gyrth's going would prevent Harold from personally confronting William in violation of the oath he had sworn two years earlier, and that, if Gyrth lost, Harold could raise another army. Harold refused to listen. By now he knew about the devastation in what had been part of his old earldom. He was determined to drive out the invaders.

Harold sent a messenger to William. He acknowledged his earlier oath but said he had been given the throne of England by Edward the Confessor on his deathbed. He told William to leave England or face destruction. William sent an answer. Harold, he said, should surrender the kingdom to him, let the pope decide between them, or settle the issue in a single, man-to-man combat with William.

William's chaplain later wrote that when Harold heard this message "he grew pale and for a long time remained as if he were dumb [unable to speak]." When William's messenger asked for an answer, Harold said, "We march at once. We march to battle. May the Lord now decide between William and me, and may he pronounce which of us has the right." Harold's shock was probably not at William's challenge, which was standard in those days, but at his messenger's news that his enemy would be fighting under the pope's banner.

Letting God Decide

Harold was an intensely religious man. He had not even known of William's mission to Rome. Perhaps now he began to think that the Norman invasion was God's punishment. This might explain why Harold would not wait for reinforcements to come from the far corners of his kingdom. Most experts agree that if Harold had waited for more troops to swell the ranks that had been depleted at Fulford Gate and Stamford Bridge, he would have won the Battle of Hastings.

But Harold would wait no longer. Possibly, after receiving word that his enemy was fighting under the pope's banner, Harold was determined to go into battle as soon as possible and let God decide between him and William. This was in keeping with the custom of trial by combat. Before juries were used to decide disputes, men frequently settled quarrels by hand-to-hand fighting. Supposedly God would give strength to whoever was telling the truth.

Harold sent word for every available, able-bodied Englishman—the great *fyrd*—to meet at the "hoar apple tree," a well-known landmark on Caldbec Hill about six miles north of Hastings. On the morning of Thursday, October 12, the king of England and his army of about four thousand men—fifteen hundred surviving housecarls and the rest from the local militias—set off for Hastings sixty miles to the south.

The army rested that night near Rochester and the next day pressed on to Caldbec Hill, arriving in the late afternoon. There

William makes camp at Hastings prior to the battle with Harold.

William in Disguise

William of Normandy was an extremely clever man. He never willingly gave away any information and tried to take advantage of every situation. This is illustrated by the deception he used on a messenger sent to Hastings by King Harold.

William was inspecting his troops when he was told that a monk, a messenger from Harold, had arrived and was seeking him. Instead of revealing himself, William said to the monk, "I am the steward of William, Duke of Normandy, and very intimate with him. It is only through me you will have an opportunity of delivering your message."

The monk gave the message, which was a demand that William return to Normandy, and the duke ordered that he be well fed and housed while a reply was prepared. The next day the monk was probably startled to see the steward seated on a throne surrounded by his nobles.

Perhaps by not immediately revealing his identity to the messenger, William was trying to trick him into saying more than he should have. A second explanation is that he merely wanted time to form a reply and pretended to be only the bearer of the message.

its numbers were increased by about three thousand, some from the trained militia, but most from the ranks of local peasants. Harold formed his troops along a ridge about eight hundred yards long to the south of Caldbec Hill. It lay across the only road north from Hastings, thus preventing the Normans from circling around. Any attack would have to come uphill.

There the English spent the night. Norman chroniclers would write later that Harold's army spent the night drinking and carousing while the Normans spent it in prayer. This was the normal sort of story written by the winners about the losers in ancient warfare, but it was ridiculous. The English had marched sixty miles in two days. Many were veterans of the Stamford Bridge battle and in the last three weeks had traveled England from one end to the other and fought a major battle in between. Doubtless, except for the sentries, they slept soundly.

Also doubtful is the theory that William surprised Harold by attacking the next morning. The armies were only six miles apart. Scouts from each side almost certainly kept their commanders informed of the other side's movements. Harold's spies reported that William was gathering for an attack. William's scouts told him they had seen two flags in the middle of the English—the Dragon of Wessex and Harold's personal banner, the Fighting Man. When he realized that Harold was facing him in person, William vowed that if given victory, he would build an abbey on the spot of the battle.

William the Conqueror was an imposing figure who had the gift of rousing complete loyalty in his troops.

William's Speech

In the predawn hours William spoke to his troops. Few physical descriptions of him have survived, but he was supposedly tall, broad, and muscular and wore his hair in the Norman fashion—medium length and shaved high up on the back of the neck. He was said to have a "harsh voice" and told his soldiers:

> Show no weakness toward [the English], for they will have no pity on you. Neither the coward for running well, nor the bold men for smiting [striking] well will be the better liked by the English. . . . You may fly [flee] to the sea, but no further. . . . The English will overtake you in your shame. More of you will die in flight than in battle. Therefore, since flight will not save you, fight and you will conquer. I have no doubt of the victory: we are come for glory, the victory is in our hands, and we may be sure of obtaining it if we so please.

Five miles from Hastings the army reached the crest of Telham Hill. From there they could see Harold's army stretched before them about a thousand yards away. Between them was a narrow valley known as the Sentlach, or "sandy area" in Anglo-Saxon. But the Normans later turned the name into Sanguelac or Senlac, or "blood lake."

Leading the invaders were the soldiers from Brittany commanded by Alan Fergant. They marched down from Telham Hill and turned left, taking up a position against the English right flank. Next came the combined troops of Flanders and France, led by Roger of Montgomerie, turning right to face the left side of the English line. Finally came the Normans, under the personal command of William, occupying the center.

The armies that faced each other were very different in their weapons and style of fighting. The English, while they might ride to the site of a battle, fought on foot. The English housecarls and select militia were armed mainly with battle-axes. These terrible weapons, capable of felling a warhorse with one blow, could be wielded with either one or two hands. The better-armed soldiers also carried spears, swords, and daggers. The peasants in the English ranks carried hunting spears or even homemade clubs. The bow as a weapon of war was not yet popular in England, so there were few archers. The professional soldiers wore chain mail and steel helmets.

The Shield Wall

The English were drawn up in a tight, defensive formation known as the shield wall. Some historians have said this meant that the shields were interlocked in some way. This is unlikely, since the soldiers would have no room to swing their axes. The shields ranged from the gaily painted, metal-reinforced shields of the housecarls to old wooden window shutters used by some of the peasants.

The Normans—at least the knights—fought on horseback independently of one another. There were no cavalry tactics, such as the use of a massed charge to break an enemy line. The knights were equipped with spears, lances, and large, heavy broadswords, and they carried long, kite-shaped shields. Like the English housecarls, they wore chain mail and helmets. The foot soldiers wore shirts of either mail or thick leather, as well as steel or leather caps, and fought with short axes or swords. There were companies of archers, but they used short bows—about four feet long—with nowhere near the range or striking power of the English longbows of later centuries. The crossbow had not yet been introduced to Europe.

Judging from his number of ships, William had crossed the channel with about ten thousand men. A few had been lost at sea, and there had likely been some casualties during the ravaging of the countryside. Also, some forces had been left with the ships to guard against an attack from sea, so William probably had about seven thousand men facing a slightly larger force under Harold.

The time was about nine o'clock in the morning, and the date, October 14, 1066, when the combatants were in place. Harold was on a black horse on the highest point of the ridge, under his two banners. Next to William was the banner given to him by the pope, and around his neck was a ring containing a relic of Saint Peter. He carried a mace, a wooden staff topped by iron spikes.

A Norman minstrel named Taillefer rode forward alone, singing and tossing his sword high in the air like a baton and catching it as it came down. He reached the English line and killed three soldiers before a battle-axe cut him down. The Norman trumpets then sounded the charge, and the Battle of Hastings had begun.

CHAPTER SIX

William in Danger

William's battle plan at Hastings was one that had served him well in all his years of warfare. However, the English infantry—mainly the housecarls wielding their battle-axes—was the finest in Europe, far better than any enemy William had faced. In the first stage of the battle William's plan quickly unraveled, and only the rashness of some of the English troops saved him from a complete defeat.

William's plan was a classic three-stage attack—artillery, infantry, cavalry—such as had been used by generals as far back as ancient Egypt. First, the archers were to pour volleys of arrows into the English line, causing both casualties and confusion. Next, the foot soldiers were to advance, taking on the enemy in hand-to-hand combat and creating breaks in the defensive formation. Finally, at just the right moment, the mounted knights were to sweep through the gaps in the line, separating the defenders into small pockets that could be surrounded and wiped out.

The plan went wrong from the very start. William's archers moved to within about a hundred yards of the English and stuck

A scene from the Bayeux Tapestry depicts the Norman invasion of England. William planned to use a classic three-stage attack to subdue Harold's troops.

their pointed, wooden quivers into the ground so they would have both hands free. Harold's men stood shoulder to shoulder, their long, oblong shields before them. The archers began to shoot but were shooting uphill. Here and there some arrows found their way through gaps between the shields, but most stuck in the seasoned wood or bounced off harmlessly. The shots that were aimed too high sailed clear over the English ranks.

Soon the Norman archers ran out of arrows. Normally they would have replenished their supply with those shot at them by the enemy. The English, however, had only a handful of bowmen in their ranks. The first stage of the attack had been completed in about a half hour, with little or no damage inflicted.

William had no choice but to send his infantry in as planned. Foot soldiers in all three divisions—Bretons from Brittany, on the left, Normans in the center, Frenchmen on the right—advanced up the hill. Before they could reach the English, a shower of missiles rained down on them: "javelins and all kinds of darts, the most murderous axes, and stones fixed to pieces of wood." The missiles took a heavy toll, but those who survived them struggled up the slope and engaged their enemy.

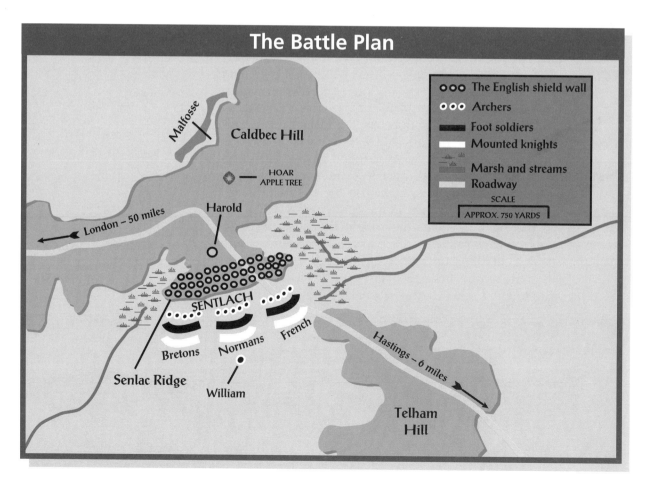

The Battle Plan

The Battle-Axes Strike

Once more the Normans were at a disadvantage by attacking uphill. Harold's housecarls were in a much better position from which to swing their huge, two-handed axes. The Normans had never faced such weapons and were shocked at the wounds they inflicted. The Bayeux Tapestry shows the bodies of several Normans, their heads completely severed despite the protection of chain mail.

The Normans and their allies, however, were seasoned troops. They fought back bravely and occasionally breached, or broke through, the shield wall. As quickly as openings appeared, however, they were filled in from the ranks just behind the front line. Above the clash of weapons—"the shock of spears, the mighty strokes of clubs, and the quick clashing of swords"—could be heard the war cries of the two sides. The Normans shouted "Dex aïe"—"God's help." The English answered with "God Almighty" and "Holy Cross," which appear in the Norman chronicles as "Godimite" and "Olicrosse."

The battle raged for an hour or more before the Normans began to retreat down the hill, followed by a hail of spears. Now it was the turn of the mounted knights to try their luck where the archers and foot soldiers had failed. The Norman cavalry galloped up the slope, but their momentum was slowed when they had to ride through their own retreating infantry. Instead of striking the English shield wall all at once, they arrived singly or in small groups. This, combined with the fact that they rode uphill, prevented the horsemen from using their charge to break through the English line.

Instead the Normans threw their spears and javelins at the English and then advanced with swords in hand. Their surviving foot soldiers followed to help. Now the full forces of both armies were in action. Few, if any, of the English housecarls, thegns, and peasants had faced mounted enemies, and many were hacked to death by the swords. The Norman losses were also heavy, as horses and men went down before the axes. The Bayeux Tapestry shows Harold's brothers, Gyrth and Leofwin, in the thick of the fight. Harold himself is pictured cleaving a horse's skull with an ax.

A scene from the Bayeux Tapestry shows Harold's troops in the first stages of victory. Norman corpses, some with heads severed, litter the ground.

Bishop Odo

It is ironic that William, a champion of church reform, would have as his strongest supporter his half brother Odo, bishop of Bayeux. Odo was a prime example of what many churchmen thought needed to be reformed.

Before William's father, Duke Robert, went on a pilgrimage in 1034, he gave his mistress, William's mother, Herléve, in marriage to Herluin, the count of Conteville. Odo was Herléve's son from this marriage.

Odo was made bishop of Bayeux at age ten, an example of how church appointments were handed out on a political basis, often to members of the ruling family. He was a staunch ally of William, pledging to give 120 ships for the invasion of England.

Bishops were expected to work for peace, but Odo was a warrior. At the Battle of Hastings he wore armor over his bishop's robe. Since a priest was not supposed to shed blood, he carried a mace—an iron-topped club—instead of a spear or sword. Presumably, clubbing an opponent to death was permitted.

After Hastings he was made earl of Kent in England. He helped William put down many a revolt. In 1080, after crushing a rebellion in which another Norman earl had been murdered, Odo had hundreds of people executed or mutilated in revenge. While he observed the ban on married clergy, he is known to have fathered at least one child.

Finally in 1082 Odo grew too ambitious. He wanted to be pope and tried to get many of his fellow Norman nobles to follow him from England to Rome. This was too much for William, who had his brother arrested, stripped of his titles, and imprisoned. He was released only on William's death in 1087 and died three years later in obscurity.

Bishop Odo says grace at a banquet after William's successful landing in England.

The Heat of Battle

This portion of the battle lasted until well past noon and was probably the fiercest fighting of the day. Casualties were high. Peasants tried to strip the armor from the dead to use themselves. One chronicle said, "Then the carnage [slaughter] was so general until past noon that neither from sharp spears, glittering lances, piercing swords, well-ground axes, nor pointed arrows, did any think to escape or to survive."

Then something happened that sent the Breton division on William's left into headlong retreat. This section of the ridge on which the English stood was narrower than the rest. Perhaps a group of Norman knights succeeded in breaking through the English, were unable to stop, and fell headlong into a deep ditch on the other side. The Bayeux Tapestry shows men and horses tumbling head over heels.

Whatever the cause, the "foot-soldiers and cavalry of Brittany, as well as all the auxiliaries who constituted the left wing, broke in flight." The retreat was a disorderly jumble. Soldiers ran over one another in their haste to escape the English axes, and horsemen trampled the soldiers. As the Bretons fled, the Normans in the center, their left flank exposed, also began to retreat.

Normans and Britons clash in fierce hand-to-hand combat during the Battle of Hastings. The Normans were surprised at the damage the Britons' battle-axes were capable of inflicting.

Harold's Position

Some military historians have criticized King Harold of England for fighting a defensive battle, not attacking William as he had Harald Hardraade at Stamford Bridge. The English position on Caldbec Hill, however, was exceptionally strong and one from which Harold could expect to wear down his opponent.

The ridge on which he massed his soldiers was about eight hundred yards long. The only road William's army could take from Hastings ran directly through it. To the south the hill descended abruptly to a level about fifty feet lower. It was up this hill that the Normans would have to attack.

In addition, there was no way for William's troops to move around to attack Harold from either side. Below the hill and about two hundred yards apart, two streams flowed in opposite directions, one to the east to the Brede River and the other to the west to the Bulverthythe River. These streams made the ground on either side of the ridge too muddy and marshy for an army to cross.

Harold's position was probably the best he could have chosen, determined as he was to have a battle. His strategy was likely one of letting the Normans wear themselves out in repeated charges and then to counterattack. Perhaps only the overeagerness of his own troops prevented his winning the battle.

With the Normans retreating, the French on the right did likewise.

In the midst of the confusion a rumor began to spread through the Normans that William was dead. The rumor filtered all the way back to the baggage carts, where the guards heard it and were ready to desert. William had to act quickly. He pulled off his helmet, showing himself to his troops. He shouted:

Look at me! I am alive and will conquer, with God's help! What madness has taken hold of you that you flee in this way? What path will lie open before your retreat? Those whom you have it in your power to sacrifice like a herd of cattle drive you back and kill you. You abandon victory and undying glory and rush headlong to your own destruction and everlasting dishonour. By flight, not one of you will escape death.

The retreat stopped and some of William's knights rallied around him.

A Critical Moment

This was perhaps the most critical moment of the Battle of Hastings. If Harold was ever to order a counterattack, this was the moment. William's army was in complete disarray. If the English had charged down from their ridge, they might well have won the battle. On the other hand, Harold might have reasoned that to pursue horsemen on foot was to invite a disaster. Once removed from their solid defensive position, the English would be at a disadvantage.

Harold decided to maintain his position, but many of his soldiers did not. Some experts have argued that perhaps Harold did order a counterattack and that part of his line started early. Most believe, however, that the troops on his right—the ones facing the Bretons—simply lost their composure. They were so excited by the sight of an enemy in flight that they could not resist going after them.

The disciplined housecarls stood firm, but hundreds of militiamen and peasants hurled themselves, screaming at the top of their voices, from the ridge in pursuit of the Bretons. William, who had gathered part of his cavalry around him, was quick to see his opportunity. He ordered his knights to wheel to their left and ride behind the advancing English, cutting them off.

At the same time Harold saw the danger and ordered his brothers, Gyrth and Leofwin, to lead a company of housecarls to rescue their countrymen. The housecarls fought bravely but were outnumbered and were fighting on foot against mounted knights. One by one they were killed, Gyrth and Leofwin among them. One account said that Gyrth encountered William, threw a

William's Gallantry

The Battle of Hastings was fought in an age when kings were expected not only to lead their armies into battle, but also to be mighty warriors, performing extraordinary feats. William of Normandy was certainly such a general. His chaplain, William of Poitiers, gave this description of William at Hastings in comparison with past heroes:

> But Duke William excelled them all both in bravery and soldier-craft, so that one might esteem him as at least the equal of the most praised generals of ancient Greece and Rome. He dominated this battle, checking his own men in flight, strengthening their spirit, and sharing their dangers.

> He bade them come with him more often than he ordered them to go in front of him. Thus it may be understood how he led them by his valour and gave them courage. At the mere sight of this wonderful and redoubtable knight, many of his enemies lost heart even before they received a scratch.

> Thrice his horse fell under him; thrice he quickly avenged the death of his steed. It was here that one could see his prowess and mark at once the strength of his arm and the height of his spirit. His sharp sword pierced shields, helmets and armour, and not a few felt the weight of his shield.

> His knights seeing him thus fight on foot were filled with wonder, and although many were wounded they took new heart. Some weakened by loss of blood went on resisting, supported by their shields, and others unable themselves to carry on the struggle, urged on their comrades by voice and gesture to follow the duke. "Surely," they cried, "you will not let victory slip from your hands." William himself came to the rescue of many.

javelin at him and missed, but killed his horse. William then rushed on Gyrth and killed him, thinking he was Harold.

With the housecarls slain, the rest of the English who had rushed from their positions on the ridge were surrounded and slaughtered. A small group gathered on a small mound. The Bayeux Tapestry shows them surrounded, poorly armed, wearing no armor, and tumbling from the mound as the Norman spears find their mark.

A Pause in the Battle

The fighting had now continued almost nonstop for four hours. Both sides were exhausted and had to rest. Even as Harold mourned the deaths of his brothers, the English carried their wounded to the rear and filled in the shield wall once more. They had lost perhaps two thousand men but still had plenty to defend the ridge. Morale was high. They had fought the invaders of their country to a standstill. They pulled their meager rations of food from pouches, washing them down with water.

William sat on a borrowed horse. His first one, a black charger given to him by a Spanish prince, had been killed, perhaps by Gyrth. He pondered what to do next. His archers had had no effect. His infantry had proved no match for the English. Even his mounted knights, the pride of his army, had been unable to break the English shield wall.

William had no choice but to renew the attack. If he retreated behind his fortifications at Hastings, Harold could surround him, blockade him from the sea, and starve him into surrender. William had risked everything on this single battle. As his soldiers rested and his archers went back to the supply wagons to get more arrows, the duke of Normandy tried to think of a new plan.

CHAPTER SEVEN

Victory and Aftermath

By early afternoon the Battle of Hastings had lasted about four hours. Thousands had been killed or wounded, yet neither William of Normandy nor Harold of England was any closer to victory. In this contest between generals it was William who devised a strategy that was to win him not only the battle, but also the throne of England.

Time was an important factor. Harold was content to reestablish his shield wall and maintain his defensive line on the ridge south of Caldbec Hill. He had suffered losses, but his strategic position was just about the same as at the start of the battle. His troops had shown that they were equal to the Normans. He also knew that he could expect reinforcements. He had left London before soldiers called from the more distant parts of his kingdom could reach him. All he had to do was maintain a standoff between the two armies, and he would eventually win.

William, doubtless, was well aware of this. He had sought a quick battle. Now that he had it, a quick victory was essential. His only source of reinforcements was across the English Channel. And for all he knew, English ships might be headed for Hastings at that very moment.

William had seen his first plan of attack fail. He knew that neither his archers nor infantry would have much of an effect against the English. He had no choice but to order the mounted soldiers to lead the next charge.

It was now about two o'clock in the afternoon, and the lull in the battle had lasted an hour. William gave orders to his lieutenants, who rode back to their divisions. A horn was sounded, and the knights charged up the hill once more. As before, they had to ride through a torrent of spears and stones before reaching the summit. The fighting was just as fierce as it had been in the morning. William was in the thick of it. Once again a horse was killed under him. He turned toward one of his knights and asked for his horse. When the frightened man refused, William reached up, seized him by the helmet, pulled him from the saddle, and rode on.

Constant Attack

There were several short pauses in this part of the battle. The Normans used them to rest, but the English could not. Each time his mounted troops pulled back, William ordered the archers to move forward and harass the enemy. The English defended themselves as before, holding their shields in front of them. The strain of being under constant attack began to wear the English down.

The Norman cavalry charged repeatedly but still could not break through the English line. Finally, after exceptionally savage fighting in the center of the ridge, the Normans began to retreat. A French writer, no friend of the Normans, later said, "Their shields covered their backs." Norman writers told a different story. They claim that William, remembering the slaughter that morning of English troops who had abandoned their position to pursue a fleeing enemy, ordered a feigned retreat. The Normans,

Mounted knight rushes uphill to charge Harold's troops. In spite of several such charges, the Normans continued to fail to break through the English lines.

they said, only pretended to retreat in order to draw the English from their shield wall.

This is the most controversial part of the battle. Norman writers were unanimous in claiming that this retreat, and one later in the battle, were part of William's strategy and were examples of his superior ability as a general. Most military historians, however, have doubted this. Communication within armies of this time period was primitive. To execute a plan such as a feigned retreat, the Norman knights, in the middle of battle, would have to pull back at the same time in response to some signal that could be heard over the uproar. Then after retreating in a body, they would have to wheel in unison to face the pursuing enemy. It is highly unlikely that William could have, without prior planning and practice, used such an intricate tactic.

What probably happened was that the English, once more, were unable to resist the urge to chase the fleeing Normans. Also, their supply of spears and javelins was probably running low, and they needed to recover some of what they had thrown down the hill. Whatever the reason, the maneuver was devastating to the English. William, surrounded by his personal guard, saw what was happening. He gathered a few hundred men and "rushed with closed ranks upon the English; and with the weight of their good horses, and the blows that the knights gave, broke the press of the enemy and scattered the crowd before them."

The Shield Wall Shortened

The number of Harold's soldiers killed in this exchange is not known, but it must have been substantial. These losses, combined with those from the renewed Norman cavalry assaults, left him with too few men to extend the shield wall the full extent of the ridge. To do so he would have spread his best troops, the housecarls, too thin and filled the gaps in between with untrained peasants. He was forced, instead, to shorten his line. The center and eastern ends of the ridge were strong, but the western end was bare. The Normans would be able to reach the top of the hill and attack over level ground.

Harold's chance for victory was gone, and he probably knew it. He could not retreat. His troops would have easily been pursued and cut down by William's horsemen. His only option was to hold on until sundown, now about two hours away. If he could, he might be able to withdraw his troops under cover of darkness and make his way back to London.

William was fully aware of this possibility. Victory was now within his grasp, and he could not afford to let it—or Harold—escape. Once again the Norman knights rode against the English. This time part of the attack came from the west side, along the ridge, in addition to the front. Still the English held.

Mounted Norman knights charge Harold's troops yet again. The knights gained a substantial advantage after they retreated and were pursued by Harold's troops. The knights were then able to turn back upon the English and kill them.

A Norman knight, Robert Fitzerneis, attempted single-handedly to kill Harold. He charged among the housecarls, heading straight for the king's banner. This lone warrior,

> grasping his shield and galloping toward the standard [banner], struck and killed an interposing [interfering] Englishman with his sword, withdrew the blade and, defying many others, pushed straight for the emblem, trying to beat it down. The English surrounding it killed him with their axes. He was found on the spot when they sought him afterwards, lying dead at the standard's foot.

The English line grew still shorter but remained unbroken. Only about an hour of daylight was left, and William had to find a way to bring the battle to an end. He decided on a final, all-out assault using all his forces. Many, if not most, of the horses had been killed, so the knights joined the foot soldiers. In what was probably his most important decision, William ordered his archers to shoot, not at the English, but high in the air, so that the arrows would come down within the enemy ranks.

A Rain of Death

The arrows "flew thicker than rain before the wind." The English in front were forced to raise their shields against the arrows, leaving their bodies exposed. When they did, the archers had a target. Other Englishmen in the rear were killed by arrows coming down on them from above.

The shield wall began to crumble. Seeing this, William ordered the charge. As arrows continued to strike the English in the rear, those in the front were once more in hand-to-hand combat with the Normans. As one account said:

> Loud now was the clamour and great the slaughter; many a soul then quitted the body. The living marched over the heaps of dead, and each side was weary from striking. He who could still charge, did so. He who could raise an arm no longer, still pushed forward. The strong struggled with the strong, some failing, others triumphing. Cowards fell back, the brave pressed on, and sad was his fate who fell in the midst, for he had little chance of rising again. In truth, many fell and were crushed beneath the throng.

Now William was able to see Harold, "fiercely hewing to pieces the Normans who were besetting him." William sent a company of twenty of his best warriors on a mission to reach and kill the king of England or die in the attempt. They hacked their way toward Harold's banner. Most were killed by the housecarls, but four reached their objective—Eustace of Boulogne (the same man who had caused the rebellion of Godwin of Wessex against King Edward), Walter Giffard, Hugh of Montford, and Ivo of Ponthieu. Hugh drove his spear through Harold's shield and into his chest. Walter struck him in the neck with his sword, sending him to the ground. As the wounded man tried to rise, Eustace pierced him through the abdomen.

Harold II, the last Anglo-Saxon king of England, fell dead, but this did not stop Ivo from hacking off one of his legs and

William's soldiers kill Harold. The bottom portion of the photo shows Harold's body being mutilated.

King Harold's Body

According to an account by Guy of Amiens, Harold's mother, Gytha, sent two monks from Waltham Abbey, which had been founded by Harold, to William. She offered to buy Harold's body for its weight in gold.

William, too, wanted the body found to make sure his opponent was dead. All the English, however, had been stripped of their armor and clothes by the Normans. William gave his permission for the monks to search, but the body had been so mutilated that the monks did not recognize it.

Gytha then sent Harold's mistress, Edith Svanneshals, to search. She found the body "by her knowledge of secret tokens which they [the monks] could not have known from his outer parts." In other words, she identified Harold's body from characteristics that only a lover would recognize.

But William did not intend for his former foe to lie in a royal tomb. He refused the gold, had the body wrapped in purple linen, and gave it to a French knight named William Mallet, who buried it under a mound of stones on a cliff overlooking Hastings.

Harold's mistress Edith searches for his body among the corpses on the battlefield.

carrying it away as a trophy. William, however, was not an unnecessarily cruel man. He respected Harold as a brave enemy. Ivo later was expelled from the army and sent back to Ponthieu without any reward.

Many later accounts of the battle said that Harold was either killed when he was struck in the eye by an arrow or was wounded in this way. This is probably because the Bayeux Tapestry, under a Latin inscription "Here, Harold the King is killed," shows a man grasping at an arrow in his eye. Also under the inscription, however, is a man whose leg is being cut off by a mounted warrior. The first chronicle to mention the arrow was written more than a hundred years later and likely came from a misinterpretation of the tapestry. The earlier version of the four horsemen is probably accurate.

The End of the Battle

With Harold dead, the English army fell apart, but the housecarls refused to surrender. They gathered into small bands, some around Harold's body, and fought on against overwhelming odds until the last man was dead.

The peasants and soldiers from the militia, however, began to scatter. Most of them fled north, with the Normans in hot pursuit. It was past five o'clock and "already the day was turning the hinge toward the shades." In the fading light the Normans failed to see a steep slope on the north side of Caldbec Hill. Unable to stop, the horsemen plunged down the hill out of control, falling atop one another in the dense brush at the bottom. The English, seeing their enemies helpless, ran back to them, killing them with daggers as they lay on the ground.

Eustace of Boulogne, leading a small company, was able to stop in time and turn back. Going back up the hill, he met William coming down. Eustace shouted at William that it was death to go on. William ordered the pursuit to continue. Just then Eustace was struck from behind by some sort of missile and knocked, wounded and bleeding, from his saddle. William changed his mind and ordered his troops back to the scene of the battle. In the gloom below, in the trench later named by the Normans the Malfosse, "evil ditch," the last of the English army finished butchering their fallen foes. Then, one by one, they slipped into the darkness of the forest. The Battle of Hastings was over.

William returned to the ridge, where a space had been cleared of bodies so that he could pitch his tent. He "ate and drank among the dead, and made his bed that night upon the field."

The next day, Sunday, the Normans buried their dead but left the bodies of the English "to be eaten by worms and wolves, by birds and dogs." William then returned to Hastings and waited to see what would happen. He expected that either a fresh army would attack him or the remaining leaders of England would come to him to surrender. Neither took place. But while William waited, he and his army were busy. Weapons were repaired. The south wind still blew and reinforcements came from Normandy, renewing the army that had lost about a third of its men. William kept his promise of founding a new abbey. He led builders onto the scene of the battle and marked out the foundations for what is now Battle Abbey, with the altar on the spot where Harold fell.

England in Confusion

The days passed, but no Englishmen appeared, either to fight or to surrender. Actually, the leaderless English could not figure out what to do. The northern earls, Morcar and Edwin, were marching toward London when they heard of the battle. They turned around and went home. An assembly met in London and elected as king Edgar the Etheling (prince), the thirteen-year-old grandson of Edmund II. The citizens of London promised to support Edgar, but the leaders of the church were less certain about him, and he went uncrowned.

Finally William decided that he was strong enough to march. He had three goals: Canterbury, the religious capital of England; Winchester, the political capital, where the royal treasury was stored; and London, the commercial capital. From Hastings he marched east up the coast to Romney, burning it to avenge two shiploads of his soldiers who had been washed ashore and killed there. From there, he moved to Dover, which his men—perhaps led by the vengeful Eustace of Boulogne—plundered.

Despite an outbreak of disease, dysentery, among his army, William moved toward Canterbury, which quickly surrendered. From the end of October to the first of November, William himself lay ill. When he was well, he marched on London but found it too strongly fortified. He passed by London to the south and went west to Winchester. Now he burned towns only when they opposed him. He wanted to rule this land, not destroy it. At Winchester the leading citizens and Harold's widow, Edith, surrendered the city.

More reinforcements, under William Fitzosbern, landed near the Isle of Wight and marched north to join Duke William. The enlarged army marched north from Winchester, crossed the Thames at Wallingford, and swung around to approach London from the north.

William the Conqueror enters London, where the citizens quickly surrender to him.

William's Coronation

William receives the crown of England at Westminster Abbey on Christmas Day.

The only record of William the Conqueror as showing fear is at his coronation as king of England. This took place on Christmas Day 1066 in Westminster Abbey.

The ceremony was not conducted by the archbishop of Canterbury, as was customary, because Archbishop Stigand had never been confirmed by the pope, a supporter of William. Instead, Archbishop Eldred of York and Bishop Geoffrey of Coutances, a Norman, officiated.

At one point in the ceremony Eldred asked the assembled crowd in English and Geoffrey in French whether they would have William as their king. The assembly, mostly Norman and French, answered with a great shout.

Norman soldiers stationed outside the church thought something had gone wrong and that William was in danger. For some unknown reason—perhaps to create a diversion—they began setting fire to the houses nearby.

When smoke began drifting into the abbey, the scene was one of total confusion. The crowd rushed out, afraid of being caught in the fire. The soldiers rushed in, thinking to rescue William, who was "trembling violently," according to one chronicler.

When order was restored, only William and a few bishops remained to complete the ceremony by which a new king of England was crowned.

The Death of William

William's victory at Hastings and his crowning as king of England was his greatest achievement. His later life, however, was anything but a case of "happily ever after."

He was to face constant rebellions and wars, both in England and in Normandy. He had to fight in Wales and in Scotland. His son, Robert, led revolts against him in Normandy with the backing of King Philip I of France. He was forced to arrest and imprison his half brother, Bishop Odo. He was reported to take little joy in life after the death of Queen Matilda in 1083.

He died as violently as he had lived. In 1087 William led his troops against the French city of Mantes, whose soldiers had been raiding across the border in Normandy. He took Mantes by surprise, slaughtered the defenders, and burned the city to the ground.

While William was riding through the ruins of Mantes the next day, a still-burning wooden beam fell, startling his horse. William was thrown violently against the front of his saddle and suffered a ruptured intestine. Six weeks later, on September 9, he died in Rouen.

Immediately after William died, it was a case of every man for himself for those who had been at his bedside. The wealthy "took to their horses, leaving rapidly to guard their property." Their servants grabbed up everything of value and followed, leaving William's body nearly naked on the floor.

William's life after his victory at the Battle of Hastings was filled with conflict, including various battles with his son, Robert. In this etching, William has been knocked off his horse in a battle with Robert.

By now the Londoners were very nervous. They had heard of the surrender of Canterbury and Winchester and all the tales of destruction of those who opposed William. When the duke and his army camped at Little Birkhamstead, about twenty miles north of the city, a delegation went out to meet them. The young Edgar was there, as were Morcar and Edwin. "They submitted from necessity," said the *Anglo-Saxon Chronicle,* "when the greatest harm had been done. It was very imprudent [foolish] that they had not done it sooner, since God, for our sins, would not remedy matters." William was asked to come to London to be made king.

On Christmas Day he was crowned in Westminster Abbey, where 877 years and twenty-nine generations later, his direct descendant, Elizabeth II, would become queen. Thanks to his victory at the Battle of Hastings, William the Bastard, duke of Normandy, had become William the Conqueror, king of England.

Importance of the Battle of Hastings

William the Conqueror's victory at Hastings had major consequences for England, both immediately and for centuries to come. Law, government, religion, architecture, and many other aspects of English life changed as a result of the Norman Conquest.

The most immediate result was widespread destruction throughout the kingdom. Although William had forced the English to accept him as king, parts of the country rebelled. Between 1067 and 1072 William put down revolts in almost every part of England. Vastly outnumbered in a hostile land, William's Norman and mercenary troops spread terror wherever they went, burning villages and crops in an effort to frighten the English into submission.

There were two reasons for the rebellions. First, William was resented by the English as a foreign conqueror. Canute, fifty years earlier, had been acceptable to much of an England that was more or less used to being ruled by the Danes. Also, Canute did not completely overturn the existing social order. Anglo-Saxon laws and customs were kept intact, and some of Canute's most trusted advisers—such as Godwin of Wessex—were English.

The second reason for the uprisings against the Normans was redistribution of land. William's Norman nobles and his French and Breton allies had to be rewarded, and William had an entire kingdom at his disposal. When William began to seize their estates, the English fought back. Eventually they were destroyed. Ten years after Hastings, only 8 percent of England was still held by members of the old Anglo-Saxon nobility.

William made an important change, however, in the way he granted land in England as opposed to the way it had been distributed both in England and in France. In both countries rulers of large areas—duchies in France, earldoms in England—had sometimes grown powerful enough to rival their kings. Now that William was himself a king, he wanted no such competition. Several great nobles were granted large amounts of land, but it was spread in small-to-medium-sized parcels throughout the kingdom. Consequently, although future English kings were frequently to face rebellious nobles, no large, virtually independent states grew up as happened in France. The comparative unity of England would contribute to its success in later wars with France.

Feudalism

Also changed was the relationship of the king to his nobles. The Normans brought the system known as feudalism to England. Under the feudal system, as opposed to that of Anglo-Saxon

A peasant shears a sheep in the shadow of the feudal manor. The Normans brought the system of feudalism to England.

England, all land was the king's. The greater nobles held their lands as fiefs, or fees, from the king and might, in turn, grant fiefs to lesser nobles, and so on down the feudal ladder to simple knights. A person holding a fief—a vassal—pledged military service to his lord. Thus, through feudalism the Normans introduced a more organized social and military system.

One aspect of feudalism, however, sowed the seeds of future trouble. William and his descendants were kings of England, but they were also vassals, as dukes of Normandy, to the kings of France. Hundreds of years later, when the interests of England and France differed and the French kings demanded obedience, the Hundred Years' War broke out. That war almost destroyed France, but it eventually made the kings in both countries stronger. The increased power of the monarchies brought feudalism to an end and laid the foundations for modern Europe.

Feudalism and landholdings had little effect on the common people. The ordinary farmers and villagers simply traded one set of masters for another. The Anglo-Saxon aristocrats, however—broken by military defeat and the loss of their lands—were virtually eliminated. Many noble families became tenant farmers on land they had formerly owned. Many former thegns, or minor nobles, went overseas, mostly to Scandinavia.

Much more important in everyday life were Norman changes in the church. Most of the bishops and abbots were replaced with Normans. Lanfranc, an Italian who had taught in Normandy, became archbishop of Canterbury in 1070. Lanfranc reformed the English church calendar, eliminating many Celtic and Anglo-Saxon saints. He also carried out the reforms being instituted by a new pope, Gregory VII. These reforms, which had been resisted by the English church up to this time, included the elimination of simony—the purchase of church offices—and the prohibition of marriage among the clergy. The effect was to bring the English church more into line with that in the rest of Europe and more under the control of the pope.

Norman Architecture

The most visible contributions of the Normans—both then and now—were their magnificent buildings. The Normans built on a grand scale, compared to which the Anglo-Saxon buildings were crude. To protect themselves in a hostile England, William's nobles built huge castles that dominated the countryside. The Tower of London was one, and William's descendants still live in another, Windsor Castle. Just as impressive are the cathedrals—such as Winchester, Durham, Salisbury—that caused the name Norman to be applied to the architecture of the time.

Another profound consequence of the Battle of Hastings was the change in the English language. Almost immediately Norman

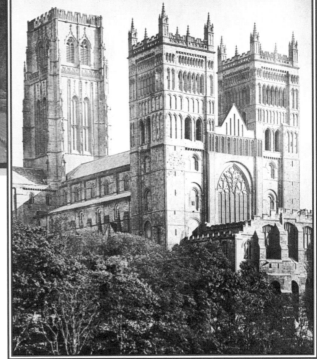

The Normans had a huge impact on English architecture. Many of their imposing structures still stand and are used today. At right is Durham Cathedral, above, Windsor Castle.

French became the language of the upper classes. English was considered crude and barbaric, something to be spoken only by peasants. Yet, English not only survived, but also in time, would produce some of the world's finest authors, including Chaucer, Shakespeare, and Milton. Much of modern English vocabulary—everyday words such as *soldier, boot, chief,* and *trail*—stems from the Norman French brought into the country by William.

The Normans kept many of the aspects of the old English legal system. They retained the shire, or county, court to hear most cases and also its chief officer, the shire reeve, or official, although the two words became combined to form the word *sheriff.* With the feudal system, however, manor courts became important as lords settled disputes between their vassals, and William appointed judges to travel around the kingdom hearing important cases, thus creating the *curia regis,* or "king's court."

The key consequence of the Battle of Hastings, and the one that made all the other changes possible, was that England became a part of Europe. Had William landed a few days earlier he would have faced a much stronger English army, one not weakened by the battles at Fulford Gate and Stamford Bridge. He might well have been defeated, and it could well have been Harald Hardraade who took the throne, instead. England would have become a Scandinavian country, influenced much more in future centuries by the laws, customs, and culture of Denmark and Norway than of France and Italy.

Had that happened, what would England be like today? Would it have spread colonies—including the United States—over the face of the earth? What would they have been like? The answers lie down that other turn in this crossroad of history. It is certain, however, that without the Battle of Hastings, the world would have been far different.

For Further Reading

Catherine M. Andronik, *Searching for the Real King Arthur*. New York: Atheneum, 1989. Traces the legends of the Anglo-Saxon hero from the standpoints of both literature and archaeology. Illustrations and photographs.

Michael Byam, *Arms and Armor*. New York: Alfred A. Knopf, 1988. Wonderfully illustrated story of how armor and weapons have changed through the centuries.

Thomas B. Costain, *William the Conqueror*. New York: Random House, 1959. Easily read story of the life of William. Almost fictional in that the author expands what little is known of some events and creates some conversations.

Kevin Crossley-Holand, *Green Blades Rising*. New York: Seabury Press, 1976. A comprehensive look at life in Anglo-Saxon England, with special attention to warfare, daily life, and religion. Photographs and illustrations, some in color. For young adults.

S. E. Ellacott, *The Norman Invasion*. London: Abelard-Schuman, 1966. The history of England from the reign of Canute through the Norman Conquest. Well-written summary for young adults. Excellent black-and-white illustrations.

Frank Hamilton, *1066*. New York: Dial Press, 1964. Good summary of the events of the year for younger grades. Good maps, but few illustrations.

Hazel Mary Martell, *The Normans*. New York: New Discovery Books, 1992. Social history of the Normans covering everyday life, dress, religion, and family life. Little about the invasion of England.

Robin May, *Alfred the Great and the Saxons*. Hove, England: Wayland Publishers Ltd., 1984. Gives the history not only of the reign of Alfred, but also of the Anglo-Saxon invasion from the beginning up to the Norman Conquest. Special attention to social life. Color illustrations and some photographs.

———, *William the Conqueror and the Normans*. New York: Bookwright Press, 1985. Excellent account of the Norman invasion and the changes it brought about in England. Color illustrations and black-and-white photographs.

Robert Nicholson and Claire Watts, *The Vikings*. New York: Chelsea House Publishers, 1994. Slim paperback volume on the conquests and way of life of the Scandinavian warriors. For younger children.

Amada Purves, *Growing Up in a Saxon Village*. Hove, England: Wayland Publishers Ltd., 1978. Looks at life in Anglo-Saxon England from the standpoints of family, home life, school, work and play, religion, and warfare. Easy to read.

Philip Sauvain, *Hastings*. New York: New Discovery Books, 1992. Short (thirty pages), easy-to-read account of the battle. Outstanding color illustrations.

R. R. Sellman, *Norman England*. New York: Roy Publishers, 1959. Not much detail on the invasion and the Battle of Hastings, but a great deal on the subsequent changes in England, including the imposition of the feudal system. Good black-and-white illustrations. For young adults.

R. J. Unstead, *Invaded Island: A Pictoral History, Stone Age to 1066*. London: Macdonald and Company, 1971. Excellent general history of Britain and England. Lavishly illustrated with color drawings, photographs, and maps.

Works Consulted

Peter Hunter Blair, *Roman Britain and Early England: 55 B.C.–A.D. 871.* New York: W. W. Norton and Company, 1963. Part of the Norton Library History of England series. A good general survey, particularly on the Anglo-Saxon invasion.

Denis Butler, *1066: The Story of a Year.* New York: G. P. Putnam's Sons, 1966. Month-by-month account of the year of the Norman Conquest. Written in an exciting narrative style, with plenty of contemporary quotations. Some maps but, oddly enough, not of the Battle of Hastings.

Christopher Brooke, *From Alfred to Henry II: 871–1272.* New York: W. W. Norton and Company, 1961. Part of the Norton Library History of England series. A well-written survey with three excellent chapters on the results in England of the Norman Conquest.

———, *The Saxon and Norman Kings.* Glasgow, Scotland: Fontana/Collins, 1967. Interesting study that deals not only with kings' dates and places, but also with changing aspects of kingship.

Edward P. Cheyney, *A Shortened History of England.* Boston: Ginn and Company, 1904. Excellent overview for the reader who wishes a short, understandable account of the basic facts.

Norman Denny and Josephene Filmer-Sankey, *The Bayeux Tapestry.* London: Collins, 1966. One of the few books in which the famous tapestry is shown in color, almost in its entirety. Accompanying the pictures is an explanatory text.

David C. Douglas, *William the Conqueror.* Berkeley: University of California Press, 1964. One of the most definitive and complete of the biographies of William. Scholarly in tone. Complete with maps and genealogical tables.

David C. Douglas and George W. Greenaway, *English Historical Documents: 1042–1189.* New York: Oxford University Press, 1968. Part of a series providing excerpts from the most important and most illustrative primary sources in English history.

H. P. R. Finberg, *The Formation of England: 550–1042.* Saint Albans, England: Paladin Books, 1977. One of the best short surveys of Anglo-Saxon England available. Good maps and genealogical charts, but no photographs or illustrations.

D. J. V. Fisher, *The Anglo-Saxon Age: c. 400–1042.* New York: Barnes and Noble, 1973. Complete account of the Anglo-Saxon invasion and its consequences on English society.

Edward Augustus Freeman, *The History of the Norman Conquest.* Chicago: University of Chicago Press, 1974. Part of the Classics of British Historical Literature series. This book, only a small part of Freeman's mammoth, six-volume series, covers only the events of 1066.

G. N. Garmondsway, translator, *The Anglo-Saxon Chronicle.* London: Dutton, 1953. Translation of all the many versions of the famous chronicle, written by various monks over the centuries, that traces the history of England, and the world, from the birth of Jesus to 1154.

David A. Howarth, *1066: The Year of the Conquest.* New York: Dorset Press, 1977. Extremely well written and readable story of the events of 1066. Much less scholarly in tone than some other versions.

David Hume, *The History of England from the Invasion of Julius Caesar to the Revolution of 1688.* Boston: Little, Brown and Company, 1854. This massive, six-volume classic of English history is now somewhat antiquated, but the section on the Anglo-Saxon era holds up well.

D. P. Kirby, *The Making of Early England*. New York: Schocken Books, 1968. Broad survey of England from the start of the Anglo-Saxon invasion to the Norman Conquest. Most of the emphasis is on social history.

Eric Linklater, *The Conquest of England*. Garden City, NY: Doubleday and Company, 1966. Excellent, highly readable survey especially valuable for its study of Scandinavian influences on both England and Normandy.

Alan Lloyd, *The Making of a King: 1066*. New York: Holt, Rinehart, and Winston, 1966. Compact, well-written story of the Norman Conquest with more attention than usual paid to Harald Hardraade's story.

Elizabeth Longford, editor, *The Oxford Book of Royal Anecdotes*. Oxford, England: Oxford University Press, 1989. A superb collection of vignettes about British and English rulers from Roman times to the present. Most are taken from contemporary sources.

D. J. A. Matthew, *The Norman Conquest*. New York: Schocken Books, 1966. A survey of the conquest that deals only briefly with the Battle of Hastings but goes into great detail about Norman rule.

Frank M. Stenton, *William the Conqueror*. New York: Barnes and Noble, 1966. A reprinting of the classic biography of William first published in 1908. Less scholarly and ponderous than might be expected even though, at five hundred pages, it goes into great detail.

George M. Trevelyan, *A Shortened History of England*. Harmondsworth, England: Penguin Books, 1962. Has been called the best single-volume history of England ever written, with good reason. Marvelous writer gives all the whos, whens, and wheres along with the hows and whys.

Dorothy Whitelock, David C. Douglas, Charles H. Lemmon, and Frank Barlow, *The Norman Conquest*. New York: Charles Scribner's Sons, 1966. A collection of four essays, each on a different aspect of the conquest. Especially valuable is Lemmon's analysis of the Battle of Hastings from the viewpoint of a military historian.

Appendix 1: The Kings of England

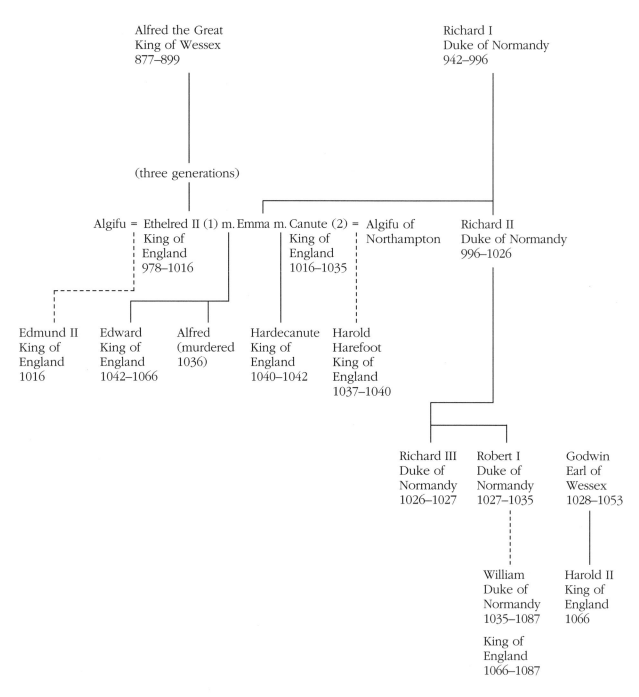

(Dotted line denotes illegitimate birth)

Parenthetical numbers indicate first or second marriages

= Equal sign indicates cohabitation

m. – marriage

Appendix 2: The Dukes of Normandy

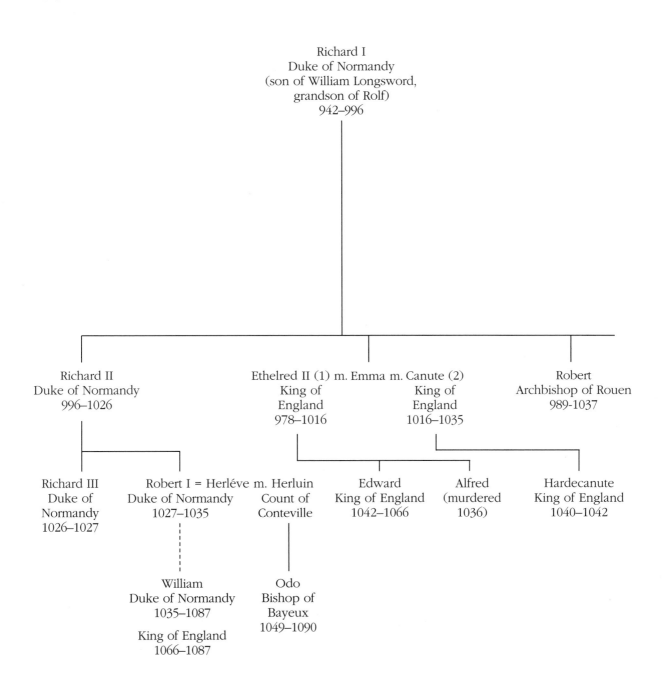

(Dotted line denotes illegitimate birth)

Parenthetical numbers indicate first or second marriages

= Equal sign indicates cohabitation

m. – marriage

Index

Picture Credits

Picture research by: Corinne Szabo

Cover photo: Stock Montage, Inc.

AKG London, 42, 74, 75

Art Resource, 22

The Bettmann Archive, 13, 14, 15, 16, 19, 26, 31, 56, 79, 85 (left)

Hulton Deutsch, 27, 51, 53

Library of Congress, 9, 11, 21, 38, 39, 43, 44, 48, 52 (both), 65, 72, 74, 85 (right)

North Wind Picture Archives, 8, 29, 30, 33, 41, 57, 59, 60, 63, 66, 67, 76, 78, 80, 83

Stock Montage, Inc., 20, 47

About the Author

William W. Lace is a native of Fort Worth, Texas. He holds a bachelor's degree from Texas Christian University, a master's from East Texas State University, and a doctorate from the University of North Texas. After working for newspapers in Baytown, Texas, and Forth Worth, he joined the University of Texas at Arlington as sports information director and later became the director of the news service. He is now director of college relations for the Tarrant County Junior College District in Fort Worth. He and his wife, Laura, live in Arlington and have two children. Lace has written several books for Lucent, including a biography of artist Michelangelo and a history of the Hundred Years' War.